Fascination
Viewer Friendly TV Journalism

Nancy Graham Holm
Aarhus
Denmark

ELSEVIER

AMSTERDAM • BOSTON • HEIDELBERG • LONDON • NEW YORK • OXFORD
PARIS • SAN DIEGO • SAN FRANCISCO • SINGAPORE • SYDNEY • TOKYO

Elsevier

32 Jamestown Road, London NW1 7BY

225 Wyman Street, Waltham, MA 02451, USA

First edition 2012

Notices

Knowledge and best practice in this field are constantly changing. As new research and experience broaden our understanding, changes in research methods, professional practices, or medical treatment may become necessary.

Practitioners and researchers must always rely on their own experience and knowledge in evaluating and using any information, methods, compounds, or experiments described herein. In using such information or methods they should be mindful of their own safety and the safety of others, including parties for whom they have a professional responsibility.

To the fullest extent of the law, neither the Publisher nor the authors, contributors, or editors, assume any liability for any injury and/or damage to persons or property as a matter of products liability, negligence or otherwise, or from any use or operation of any methods, products, instructions, or ideas contained in the material herein.

British Library Cataloguing-in-Publication Data

A catalogue record for this book is available from the British Library

Library of Congress Cataloging-in-Publication Data

A catalog record for this book is available from the Library of Congress

ISBN: 978-0-12-416037-8

For information on all Elsevier publications
visit our website at elsevierdirect.com

This book has been manufactured using Print On Demand technology. Each copy is produced to order and is limited to black ink. The online version of this book will show color figures where appropriate.

Working together to grow libraries in developing countries

www.elsevier.com | www.bookaid.org | www.sabre.org

ELSEVIER **BOOK AID International** Sabre Foundation

Drawings by Niels Gorm Andersen

To
Hannah and Hans-Henrik

Contents

Preface

A New Curriculum for a New Era

Increased commercialisation in television broadcasting has brought unprecedented change in viewing. Where once a nation's public service broadcast industry reigned supreme with a monopoly of viewers, now there is competition from other channels whose programming is commercially sponsored, either wholly or partially. Competition for an audience is now a common element for survival in the television industry.

TV journalism has not escaped this competition and broadcasters have been forced to upgrade production values in order to attract and hold viewers. This is particularly true if informative programmes want to attract and keep the attention of young people, often referred to as the "MTV generation," instinctively intolerant of slow paced, unimaginative audio and video. Unconsciously, this audience experiences pictures and sound on a *sensory* level. They *feel* the communication and when they can't *feel* it, they often tune out.

Historically speaking, it was print journalists that invented TV news and it is not surprising that they gave little attention to television as a visual medium. Today, the medium has matured and there are creative alternatives to "rip and read" wordy voice-over-pictures. Prejudices, however, die slowly. Television journalists who come from the print medium are often slow to recognise the journalistic value of pictures and natural sound. To them words compose the heart of journalism and pictures are merely *illustrations*. Television pictures move, yes, but they are still just illustrations.

In addition, many senior journalists who grew up in newspaper and magazine journalism are unconsciously suspicious of pictures and sound. They know they are emotional while words are intellectual. This attitude is what keeps television journalism from exercising its potential, locking it into a concept that can best be described as "radio with pictures."

It is not difficult to understand this prejudice. Words *are* "intellectual" compared to pictures/sound and journalists who take themselves seriously as professionals do not want to manipulate the viewer emotionally. As a result, many TV journalists choose a style of storytelling that is wordy and long-winded, fearing that pictures and sound when left alone might be misinterpreted. In addition, some journalists hate to miss an opportunity to tell "just one more fact."

An alternative point of view, however, suggests that prudent and judicious use of pictures with natural sound can inform just as well as words. Indeed, creative use of pictures and natural sound can elevate TV journalism from mere reporting to storytelling.

Television journalism is not entertainment, of course, nor should it try to be. If one agrees that professional journalism is essential to democracy, however, then it follows that knowledge of these new *sensory* techniques is necessary in order to apply them judiciously and appropriately to informational programming. Techniques change fast while creating new standards. Journalism schools that teach television need not only to keep pace but also to stay ahead of the standard.

Since the early 90s, The Danish School of Media and Journalism (DSMJ) has designed its curriculum to be on the cutting edge and this book is an initiative to share this information with other European schools and their colleagues throughout the world where TV journalism is taught. It could well be interpreted as a contribution to the so-called Bologna Process by which educational "best practices" are moving toward harmonisation. The techniques in this book are offered, therefore, as an alternative to traditional practices. It does not mean that traditional practices are "wrong," only that there is room for innovation.

Generally speaking, this curriculum is Anglo-American and a blend of three pedagogical concepts:

1. the British-North American signposting model for "top down" information-based *reporting*;
2. TV's adaptation to narrative journalism, called "eye level" *storytelling*; and
3. principles of media aesthetics that give technical fascination to TV journalism.

The British-North American model of *reporting* has been around for decades but is not often practiced outside the UK. It is, however, similar to the Danish concept of *berettermodellen* and is recognised and encouraged by the trainers at DR, Denmark's original public service channel.

Storytelling as opposed to reporting is the heart of "people stories." They differ very much from traditional TV journalism and challenge conventional norms about how much information is necessary to inform.

A systematic discussion of media aesthetics is seldom a part of European TV journalism education. Here it is incorporated throughout the curriculum to reinforce technical standards, enhance *fascination* and give legitimacy to the Anglo-American ideas of the craft.

Admittedly, several of the terms and concepts are not conventional but invented by the author. "Harry Potter edits," "BBI," "A-V tease," "the chocolate rule," "TTT," "Piaf" and a "good talker" are examples.

The curriculum itself has evolved over a fifteen-year period. It was originally designed to teach senior students and has been offered as standard pedagogy since 1993. In 2004, DSMJ established an international TV class and since then, journalism students from Spain, Italy, Slovakia, Estonia, Latvia, Lithuania, Germany, The Netherlands, Greenland, Sweden, Russia, Norway, Ethiopia, Nepal and Finland have participated in a 15-week course using it. In addition, many of the techniques have been exported since 1995 through consultancies to Albania and France as well as guest teaching in Mongolia and Slovakia.

Who can use this book? Although many of the basic principles are included in this book, it is not an introduction to TV journalism. The scope is deep not wide and is intended to be supplementary to standard textbooks. It is designed to inspire reflection about engagement and to instil an appreciation of aesthetic fascination. A glossary at the end helps to define the relevant terms.

Nancy Graham Holm

Acknowledgments

I spent the first 5 years of my life at radio station KOA (Denver), confined to safe places while my father read the news and my mother used her voice to play parts in various radio dramas. Thus, it might be fair to say that I was born into broadcasting, with a special relationship to voices and sound. To this end, I must acknowledge my parents who were the first to teach me technical fascination.

After that, the list is long. It starts with two teachers at San Francisco State University, Herb Zettl and Stuart W. Hyde. They convinced me that television was more fascinating than radio, and if my father never forgave them for this treachery, they nevertheless started his daughter on a journey that began in community affairs at KTVU (Oakland) and finished 35 years later in Scandinavia. Professor Zettl opened my eyes and ears to media aesthetics, and Professor Hyde introduced me to significant vision. Thank you, gentlemen.

After 20 years in journalism, my education started again when I left the field to enter the classroom. I am grateful to two Vice-Chancellors, Peter Kramhøft, who invited me, a North American, to teach in Denmark, and later, Kim Minke, who asked me to write this book. Thank you for your confidence.

I am also indebted to three of my colleagues at The Danish School of Media and Journalism who supported my efforts to learn how and why TV journalists do what we do. Jette Sachs gave a voice to the concepts of focus and the sharply angled story while remaining a loyal coconspirator in the battle to honor information-based reporting. Jørgen Torp created pedagogy for voice-overs and writing for the ear while sustaining me for 14 years with his unfailing humor. Henrik Laier was the first to challenge my prejudices about "eye-level" storytelling and to help me appreciate its value. Thank you my friends.

Learning how to teach TV journalism has been a family project, and special gratitude goes to Lotte Holm and Rikke Holm for their patience and counsel in the early years, when every word in a story needed to be translated before it could be evaluated; also to Mikkel Holm for sharing my passion for sound.

Finally, I wish to acknowledge my students from 1991 to the present: Danes, mostly, but also Estonians, Slovakians, Norwegians, Spaniards, Russians, Italians, Swedes, Nepalese, Lithuanians, Dutch, Finns, Latvians, Czechs, Ethiopians, Germans, Mongolians, French, Americans, and Canadians. They are the ones who taught me how to teach. Many of them read this book in its early drafts and were quick to tell me when things didn't work. Other helpful feedback came through international consultancies for The European Broadcasting Union in Geneva and the European Journalism Centre in Maastricht.

Repairs and refinements have been made and I am grateful to Professors Frederick Shook and Herbert Zettl for their careful reading of later versions and unfailing support and suggestions. The responsibility for any errors or misconceptions is entirely my own.

1 Overview

A mantra for effective TV journalism might well be: *Information-Identification-Fascination.*

Information is the easy one because this is what journalists do: we inform. What is not always obvious, however, is how much information is necessary to inform. How many facts? How many experts? How much analysis? And is information the only way to inform?

Identification means we produce for our target audience. We try to communicate with as many people as we can and this is what separates journalists from artists.

What is new, however, is that some forms of contemporary journalism make a priority of *identification* over information.

Fascination emphasizes engagement. By emotionally attaching the viewer to the story, information is easier to understand and more importantly, easier to remember. Technically, this is achieved through the sensory experience of using sight, sound and motion. Journalistically, it is achieved through style, story structure and the role of the TV journalist.

It is *fascination* that is the subject of this book.

Natural Sound and Articulate Pictures

Throughout much of Europe, the traditional practice for *information-based* stories is to limit the audio track to a voice-over (VO) narration and segments from interviews. These are typically lengthy (25–45 seconds) and when there are several in a row, the story starts to resemble radio. Anglo-American industry practitioners rudely label this type of TV journalism "radio with pictures."

As an alternative, when interview segments are short (7 to 15 seconds), the journalist tells the story with visual proof, using articulate pictures and natural sound.

Articulate pictures emphasize composition; a respect for vectors; sequential pictures; appropriate exposure; editing on movement; "shoot 'n move" to get new angles; and primary motion instead of secondary (pans, zooms or tilts) unless it is motivated.

Natural sound is not limited to objects or animals but includes segments of conversations from fly-on-the-wall reportage. We want to hear dogs bark, car doors slam, tractor engines roar, water slosh, birds chirp and motorcycles go baroorooooom! We also want to hear the "private" comments between the two guys on the fishing boat, the two shoppers in the department store or the policemen at the demonstration.

The paradox is that sound is what gives pictures their power. So important is this concept that throughout this book, the term will be written in uppercase letters: NATURAL SOUND. Since we are not talking about radio, however, it is understood

Fascination. DOI: 10.1016/B978-0-12-416037-8.00001-8

that NATURAL SOUND is always accompanied by video images. A shorthand way of expressing this is A-V for audio-video. Examples of story treatments, therefore, will ask for an A-V tease at the top of the story, A-V transitions *between* points and chapters, and A-V "bites" *inside* points and chapters. These concepts are discussed extensively in Chapters 2, 3, 5–9.

Story Styles

Journalistically, this book does not address news bulletins (:45–1:30) but the "developed" story including the mini-documentary and long documentary (2:30–5:00–8:00–30:00), stories that are categorised as *current affairs*. The challenge is to make these stories viewer-friendly by enhancing fascination.

The stories are self-contained; developing and unfolding in a systematic fashion with a beginning, middle and an end. In some industries, they're called a "package" and do not require the studio presenter to give 15% of the information. Instead, studio introductions merely "tease" the story and prepare the viewer for what is coming.

Chapter 4 is devoted entirely to story *treatment* with attention to the various proportions of information to fascination. *Information-based* stories are distinguished from *features*. In addition, there is the third category that we call *people stories*.

The first story type is told *top down* and unfolds through *reporting*. The second type is not told top down by the journalist, but from *eye level* through people and unfolds through *storytelling*.

Top down stories are told from the outside looking in. Eye level stories are told from the inside looking out. The first is relatively intellectual. The second is relatively emotional. These concepts are discussed in Chapters 5–7.

The Role of the TV Journalist

Fascination doesn't stop with technical and journalistic skills, however. An additional element to a viewer-friendly story is the face behind the voice. Should the TV journalist show up on the screen? If yes, in what ways? Is personality a variable and is it appropriate to TV journalism? This question is discussed in Chapter 10.

New Options, New Challenges

Making a story "viewer-friendly" is significant because *we should never assume that viewers remember what the journalist knows*. Predictably, there will be some who say that what is offered in this book cannot be applied in real life. They will say that the demands of a real newsroom make many of these techniques a luxury and that *"there is no time"* to do the things it suggests.

Since we know, however, that these techniques are standard practices in North America and parts of the United Kingdom, perhaps the solution to time pressures is finding new ways to organise production teams.

Here is a summary of what is to follow:

- *Treatment*: what is the topic? Does it merit development? Is it a picture story? What is the best angle to inform? How much information do we want to give? Is it an information-based story or a feature? If identification is more important than information, perhaps the story should be treated from eye level. This will require a case study as a central character. Do we have time to find one? How long should the story be?

- *The story has a beginning, middle and an end:* information-based stories use signposting, which we call the Triple T Design. TTT asks for: tell me what you want to tell me. Tell me. Tell me what you told me. Features have a more flexible structure but work best when they also go from the general to the specific and then back to the general. *People stories* involve a strong central character engaged against opposition towards a specific goal.

- *Interviews in short information-based stories are used only as documentation:* interviews do not tell the story but serve merely as evidence to support the claims of the reporter. The opposite is true for features and people stories in which the interviews can tell much of the story, providing the subjects are good storytellers.

- *Natural sound:* the audio track is emphasized throughout all stories in order to give *presence* to the story and allow the viewer to *experience* what is going on.

- *The video is planned:* the photography uses a blend of fly-on-the-wall reportage, constructed pictures and infrequently, re-constructions. If the story is recorded under controlled conditions, it is choreographed, using *sequential* shots, including wide shots, medium shots and close-ups, photographed from various angles. *Pans, zooms and tilts are avoided unless they are motivated*. Pictures are shot with a tripod unless the camera operator can shoot hand-held with stability. A shooting script offers the journalist a map and a guide to what pictures are needed.

- *The editing is also planned:* an editing script is written only after all the photography is reviewed. The script makes room for pauses of A-V bites in the VO narration. If sequential shots were recorded involving movement, the pictures are edited *on* the movement by overlapping action.

- *A-V transitions:* NATURAL SOUND and pictures between story points or chapters tell the viewer what is coming next.

2 Sound

There are five types of sound in TV journalism:[1]

- Sound from the pictures
- Voice-over narration (VO)
- Edited segments from interviews (SYNCS)
- Journalist to camera
- Music
- Room tone

Sound from pictures can be of two types: (1) the sound of objects such as doors slamming, dogs barking or feet walking on wet leaves. When not simultaneously recorded, such sounds can be edited from sound effects.

(2) People sounds recorded independently of interviews.

NATURAL SOUND is what this is called; sounds from the environment that serve to heighten the viewers' sense of realism. It is the auditory part of the visual experience and normally recorded simultaneously with the pictures.[2]

A common way of recording NATURAL SOUND is fly-on-the-wall. This technique asks the camera and microphones to "spy" on people, recording them ostensibly without their awareness. (Unless the camera and microphones are hidden, however, it is usually with their permission.)

NATURAL SOUND allows the viewer to *experience* an event. Picture a beach with crashing waves that you can't hear. You only *see* them. Half of the experience is lost without the sound. Paradoxically, sound gives pictures their power. The audio track is what enhances the photography and gives pictures their ability to communicate.

In real life, dogs bark, car doors slam and motorcycles go barooroooom! Football players grunt and spectators at sports arenas yell and cheer. Why is it that we seldom hear these sounds in TV journalism stories? "Oh, it's there! You just can't hear it!" is what we are often told. In the haste of getting the story produced, the editor was happy just to get the VO narration linked with the pictures and to insert the interview bites.

Some editors will say that NATURAL SOUND interferes with the VO narration. This might well be true, if the pictures are edited first. If the voice track is edited before the pictures, however, the editor can plan for the pauses in which A-V bites will enhance the story. Digital editing makes it especially easy.

---

[1] VOs are discussed in chapters 5,6, and 7; interviews in chapter 9 and the role of the TV journalist in chapter 10.
[2] North American TV journalists refer to this as "nat sound." Another term is ambient sound. In the UK, the term *actuality* is more commonly used.

Fascination. DOI: 10.1016/B978-0-12-416037-8.00002-X

When giving consideration to NATURAL SOUND, keep these principles in mind:

- Stop talking!
- Let the pictures and sound breathe!

If all we hear is wall-to-wall VO and lengthy interviews, we can't connect to the story emotionally.

NATURAL SOUND makes the story more engaging.

Engaging stories are easier to understand. Engaging stories are easier to remember.

Natural Sound Gives Information

Pictures are units of visual information. Short segments of NATURAL SOUND are units of auditory information.[3]

Example: CNN did a profile of Timothy McVeigh, the man who blew up the U.S. Federal Building in Oklahoma City in 1995. The subject of the profile was locked up in jail and not available for interviews. As an alternative, CNN did deep research on McVeigh's background and then used pictures and NATURAL SOUND to describe his childhood, adolescence and life as a soldier in the US Army.

The opening shots show an ordinary American high school football game with cheerleaders *("Two-four-six-eight! Who do we appreciate?")* and gum-chewing teenage girls *(pop!)* in the audience. Other shots show bingo games *(C 4! Tumble tumble H 7!)* and an abandoned factory with a rusted window frame flapping in the wind. *(Creeeak!)*. Later, we go to basic training at Fort Bennington, Georgia and crawl under barbed wire with the new recruits and on long road marches with heavy backpacks. Close-ups of combat boots go *(stomp stomp stomp!)* Automatic weapons fire bullets, *(tet tet tet!)* Men grunt and yell as they crawl under barbed wire. *(Mad dog!)* These are strong images that emphasise militarism. The journalist intervenes at various points and adds information in the VO, yet 35% of the story is told without words.

This is television story telling at its best. It is information-intensive but not because of the words.

The Ear Expects to Hear Sound

Another reason to use NATURAL SOUND is to give the viewers what they expect. The human ear expects to hear sound when dice are thrown across a wooden table or when wine is poured into a decanter. When dogs bark open mouthed on the

---

[3]A "sound-bite" is a very brief segment of an interview. In Europe, some industries use this term to mean natural sound and it is, apparently, a misapplication of English. In order to assure clarity throughout this book, we will use two terms: *sound bite* for interviews and *A-V bite* for natural sound and pictures.

TV screen yet nothing is heard, it is unconsciously disconcerting because it is not normal. *Always record NATURAL SOUND and lay it under the VO when editing. Allow for pauses in the VO and then bring up A-V bites when the ear expects it.* This adds a rich contextual flavour to the pictures.

Example: the story is about mushroom collecting in the woods during autumn. When people walk in the woods, their feet make a **crunch crunch** sound. Record it and use it! The story will be just a little richer for hearing the sound of feet on autumn leaves. The same can be said for horses' hooves on gravel or the blades of a sledge on snow.

An A-V Tease Introduces the Story

Before the VO narration starts at the top of a story, use :02 to :04 of natural sound to tell the viewer what the story is about. This prepares the viewer to receive the spoken information.

Example: the story is about politicians who use tax-payers' money for foreign travel. We come up from black to a long shot (LS) of a commercial airliner taking off and NATURAL SOUND of a jet engine. ***Roooooooooaaaar!*** VO: Too many politicians travel on taxpayers' money.

Example: the story is about street crime in a particular neighbourhood. We come up from black to a medium shot of a police car with NATURAL SOUND of its siren. ***Ha HEEha Hee ha Hee ha!*** VO: This is what you hear almost every night in Greensboro Heights.

Example: the story is about the hot new Danish fashion industry. We come up from black to a clothes rack. In a medium close-up (MCU), we see dresses on hangers moved by a hand and hear ***scraaape!*** of the hangers on the metal rack. VO: Move over Armani! Make room for Vero Moda!

A-V Bites Reinforce Significant Points

Consider a door that slams shut. This can be used to creatively underscore a point in the VO narration.

Example: VO: Union members voted on Friday to reject the new contract. They will stay on strike until their demands are met. ***SLAM!***

A-V Transitions Link Points and Chapters

All TV journalism stories have chapters or segments. An effective tool for bridging them is a medium close-up (MCU) with natural sound.

Example: the story is about an American teenage girl in a European school. The story starts with her family life then cuts to her school and then to the sports field. The bridges between the three segments are A-V transitions.

Thus, we leave our subject sitting in a long shot (LS) at the dining table with her European family. We edit to a MCU of a teacher's arm at the blackboard and hear *fly-on-the-wall*. *"Most of you got this wrong. The square root of the problem is…." (teacher talks about a maths problem mixed with the sound of the chalk, :04).* We cut away to a medium close-up (MCU) of the American girl sitting in the class and looking confused. Now we know that the focus of the new segment is "school life." We can continue the story with VO narration from the reporter, an interview bite or VO from the subject herself.

After this segment is finished, we want to tell about the girl's interest in sports. We bridge "school" with "sports" in a similar way. We hard cut to an extreme close-up (XCU) of a football. It is kicked out of the frame with NATURAL SOUND: *whooosh!* We cut to a long shot of the playing field and establish our subject playing European football, recorded fly-on-the wall. We inter-cut to a medium shot (MS). Now we know the focus of this segment is sports. We can continue the story with VO narration from the reporter, an interview bite or VO from the subject herself.

Natural Sound Works Well with Split Audio

Sometimes referred to as an L cut in digital editing, this technique separates picture and sound, allowing us to hear something before we see it. It is often used on interviews by allowing us to hear the subject's voice before we see a face. L cuts are also used effectively with NATURAL SOUND.

Example: a tour guide in a Berlin cemetery is talking about *Kristallancht*, the historic evening in 1938 when citizens attacked Jewish businesses. The sounds of a steam train fade up as the tour guide finishes his comments and people walk away through the cemetery. After 3–4 seconds of train sounds *(CHOO cho cho!)* we cut to railroad tracks and the story continues with commentary about the Holocaust.

The same technique can be used with a wide variety of natural sounds. Crickets in the summer. Wind during a storm. A police siren. A crowd of people at a circus. Traffic sounds. A child crying. A horse whinnying.

Natural sounds make good television transitions.

Best practice:
Use natural sound as transitions

Use Music to Set an Emotional Tone

Compared to pictures, which are perceived through the eyes and relatively intellectual, music is perceived with the ears and is relatively emotional. Experiments have been conducted using identical pictures with different music and the perceived message can be 180 degrees apart.

Many stories are enhanced by music, but choose carefully. Using an inappropriate melody can sabotage the story.

Beware of Edith Piaf!

A common mistake is to edit music with lyrics under a VO or segments of an interview. This requires the viewer to listen simultaneously to two sets words on two different subjects.

Example: the story is about African immigrants in Paris and opens with panoramic beauty shots of the Eiffel Tower. Gradually we move to the appropriate neighbourhood and get a feel for the environment through fly-on-the-wall photography. Over the opening shots, Edith Piaf sings her famous *Sous le ciel de Paris.*

> *S'envole une chanson, Hum Hum*
> *Elle est née d'aujourd'hui*
> *Dans le coeur d'un garçon*
> *Sous le ciel de Paris*

The first 15 seconds are delightful! Piaf's extraordinary voice sets the tone perfectly but then the reporter starts to speak in a VO and our ears must comprehend a blend of two languages and two sets of words. Would it help if the VO was also in French? Probably not. In fact, this might make it even more confusing. French, English, German, Slovakian, Dutch, Spanish? Danish? No matter what language the reporter is speaking, our ears hear two different components of information.

Music with lyrics is effective if used alone. Otherwise, use *only the melodic parts* under VOs and sound bites from interviews.

Best practice:
Don't mix music lyrics with VO or interview SYNCS

Natural Sound or Music?

Working with NATURAL SOUND is demanding. Sometimes documentary producers give up and simply lay in music. Maybe music is just what the story needs. Other times, however, it is obviously a lazy way to give pictures an audio track. The best solution is a blend of music to set an emotional tone and A-V bites to take us closer to the experience.

Walla

This is a sound effect for the murmur of a crowd in the background. The word was created in the old radio days when they needed the sound of a crowd and they found if several people simply repeated *"walla, walla, walla, walla"* it sounded like people talking. The audience did not really hear the words, just the buzz of the voices.[4]

Room Tone

This is the ambient sound peculiar to each separate environment that is inserted into editing to prevent sound dropouts. It is the recorded sound of a room that is the result of mere vibrations in the air. No room is absolutely "dead" and segments of "room tone" are edited to avoid "dead air" between interview segments.

Best practice:
Record room tone

Microphones are Stupid!

The microphone records whatever and whomever it hears. Some excellent fly-on-the-wall material has been ruined by the wrong voices on the track, example: *"Hey Jesper, isn't it time for lunch?"* Other sound tracks have been ruined by the *scrape, scrape* of fabric from the interview subject's clothing or the *clink clink* of a necklace.

---

[4] Instead of *walla, rhubarb* is used in the UK.

Best practice:
Wear headphones when recording

3 Articulate Pictures

Radio stories rely on NATURAL SOUND and descriptive language to open the imagination of the perceiver. Television uses pictures, which become part of the *communication*. Pictures in TV journalism are not just merely images, however. They have to say something. They have to be articulate.

Avoid Wallpaper Video

This is American slang referring to pictures with relevance yet little meaning to the main point of the story. They are close enough to the subject, however, that they might be interpreted as illustrations. Wallpaper video is usually the result of lazy work.

Two Types of Pictures for Storytelling

Basically, there are two types of pictures: *"illustrative"* and *"sequential."* The *illustrative* style is the most frequently used style in television news. As deadlines become increasingly tighter, producers and editors rely on this style as the most efficient method of telling a story. Pictures are illustrations of what the words say in the VO.

"Sequential" pictures are more cinematic than illustrative pictures because they use a variety of different sized shots such as we see in feature films. Sequential video produces a continuous, uninterrupted flow of action that tells the story. Sequential pictures are like a family of shots: The establishing shot is the father. The medium shots are the mother and all the close-ups are the children. Like a family, they relate to one another. They are edited together to move the story forward.

Fly-on-the-Wall Photography

Also called *vérité*, this is a style of shooting that may serve as either illustrative or sequential. It is characterised by watching the action unnoticed, like a fly on the wall. It is sometimes used interchangeably with *reportage,* although *reportage* itself is a larger concept.

When people talk in fly-on-the-wall photography, they never speak to the camera or to a journalist. They talk to one another and the photographer is "invisible."

Fascination. DOI: 10.1016/B978-0-12-416037-8.00003-1

Visual Proof

Both types of pictures – *illustrative* and *sequential* – provide *visual proof* in TV journalism. Visual proof is the essential difference between television and radio.

The viewer expects to see what the VO is talking about.

Example: the story is about the Danish fashion industry and how large-scale exports to North America are changing fashion trends. *"Modern Danish textile design is cool,"* the reporter says. *"Dresses, skirts and tops are different and creative. They're expensive but some say they're worth it!"*

Television journalism is a visual medium and this particular story *is* visual. Now the viewer expects to *see* examples of these fashion statements. Unless there are examples, the story falls flat. It is not enough to have a journalist or interviews *tell* us that the clothes are cool and different. The viewer has to *see* that they are.

Best practice:
Show me! Don't tell me

Example: the story is for a foreign audience about the 190% surtax on the sales price of automobiles in Denmark.

The opening shot must have visual evidence of "cars" and "Denmark." An ordinary highway picture of bumper-to-bumper automobiles could be anywhere. How about a medium close-up of cars in mid-town parked next to bright red Danish post boxes? Or as an alternative: the back end of a car with the bright blue European Union decal with stars and "DK" in the middle? Now we have visual proof.

Example: the story is about Lithuanian doctors that emigrate to Copenhagen where they can earn eight times the salary for the same work.

It is not enough to hear them talk about it. We need *visual proof* of the differences in their lifestyles. In Copenhagen, we need to *see* them in their leisure time, going to concerts, the theatre etc. We need to *see* them as consumers, buying more than food and living space. In Vilnius, we need to *see* them working at two and three jobs just to buy necessities and pay rent. We need to *see* the quality of their lives.

If the participants refuse to let you videotape their lives and insist on keeping the recording to just interviews, you will end up with a very good radio programme. Television requires *visual proof.*

Different Shots, Different Sizes

Long shots are taken from a far distance. They are either ordinary long shots (LS) or extreme (XLS). Long shots are used to tell where the story is happening and are sometimes called establishing shots (ES). Establishing shots are always some type of long shot but they do not necessarily have to be the very first shot in the story.

A close-up (CU) is anything seen at close range that fills up the screen. It can be loose (MCU) or tightly framed (CU) or extremely close (XCU). A medium shot (MS) is anything between a long shot and close-up.

Shoot 'n move! Shooting sequences (example: wide shots to medium shots to close-ups) work best when the *angle* on each shot is changed. A new angle gives the edit more energy.

Primary and Secondary Motion

Video images that are shot without moving the camera body or the lens are called *primary motion* shots. Any movement that is in the pictures comes from the subject itself.

Pictures that use pans, tilts, zooms or trucking movements are called *secondary motion* shots. The movement in the pictures comes from the camera body or lens, regardless of what the subject is doing.

Before the invention of the variable lens, storytelling in pictures used long shots, medium shots and close-ups that were shot with different lenses. This made the stories interesting and cinematic. Then the variable lens was invented and TV photographers got lazy. A high percentage of European TV news stories are told through pans, zooms and tilts. An alternative is though primary motion.

Use Secondary Motion Only When it Is Motivated

There should be a reason for the secondary motion.

Example: a highway is planned that will run dangerously close to a school playground. The only way to show how close they are to one another is by panning.

Editing Primary and Secondary Motion Shots Together

There is a rule for editing primary and secondary motion shots together. Specifically: secondary motion shots must come to a complete stop before they can be cut to a primary motion shot. Ignoring this rule means that the viewer experiences a sinking feeling in the pit of his stomach.

Any secondary motion shot can be cut to any other secondary motion shot, however, without coming to a complete stop. In other words: any pan, zoom, tilt or trucking shot must come to a complete stop before cutting to a primary motion shot. Any pan, zoom, tilt or trucking shot, however, can be cut to any other pan, zoom, tilt or trucking shot at any point regardless of motion.

Best practice:
STOP!
Make the pan (zoom, tilt) come to rest before editing to a picture that is not moving

Different Types of Photography

Most stories, regardless of their length, are produced with a blend of picture types. Sometimes a story will need re-constructed pictures and then we need to tell the viewers that what they are watching is fabricated.

Fly-on-the-wall reportage is what the TV photographer shot at a specific event where the action cannot be controlled. Action at certain events happen only once and a skilled TV photographer will "get it" with as many primary motion shots as possible, hopefully with some sequences. If the action is fast and dangerous, the pictures will often be shot in secondary motion. When writing the VO narration, a skilled TV journalist will look at the visuals and listen to the NATURAL SOUND and ask: what do these pictures *make* me say? (See Chapter 8 on Words versus Pictures).

Example: in 2004, Chechen terrorists held 300 hostages in a Beslan school. The hostages were mainly children, while their parents waited outside the buildings. The pictures were pure *reportage.* Nothing was constructed.

Constructed pictures are the ones that we need to *illustrate* what we say in the VO narration. We must photograph specific shots to illustrate specific points.

Example: the story is about "Hans," who plans to roller skate to Paris from Copenhagen in order to make a political statement. He wants the law to be changed to give skaters the right to use bicycle paths. He hasn't done it yet. He is merely planning to do it. We write the script to tell the story and then we make a "shopping list" of pictures that we need to illustrate it.

Here is part of our list:

1. LS, MS, MCU and CU of Hans skating: on the road; in his neighbourhood; through the park.
2. CUs and MCUs of his legs and skates.
3. A map that will show the route he intends to take.
4. NATURAL SOUND of roller skates on tarmac.

Framing the shot: use the technique of still photographers to frame their pictures by making a rectangle with your fingers. Raise your left hand with the palm outwards. Raise your right hand with the palm inwards. Attach your thumbs to your index fingers, close one eye and then look through the "box" to frame your shot.

Re-constructed pictures are the re-enactment of certain events to illustrate specific points in the script.

They are not "fiction" in that they correspond to actual events. Viewers have the right to know when pictures are reconstructions and keying a graphic indicates this by saying: "dramatisation" or "reconstruction."

Example one: the story is about a murder that took place twenty-five years ago. The producer hires actors to re-enact the event. Perhaps the colour is removed from the pictures to emphasise the re-enactment and to make it more emotional.

Example two: the story is about the historical Jesus. Who was he? What did he look like? How much can we rely on scientific evidence when we talk about his life after death? If budget permits, the producer hires actors in costumes to re-enact events. Historical re-enactments are obvious to viewers and do not require a text on the screen that says: "reconstruction."

CUs Need a Context for Reference

Example: Tivoli Gardens in Copenhagen has several fountains. Unless we use a long shot (LS) to establish the context of the fountain, a close-up (CU) of the fountain alone does not make sense. Close-ups are details of the bigger picture and details need a context.

CUs as Effective Transition Shots

Example: in a variety of long shots, cowboys round up cattle and a beautiful girl rides along just for the experience. In a CU, a cowboy smiles at her. In a reverse CU, she smiles back. Now what? The story needs to move ahead. We can use one more long shot of the two of them on horseback and then we can cut to an XCU of the campfire and his boot as he strikes a match on his heel. They have moved from their horses and are in a new setting. Now the story can move forward.

The Tighter the Shot, the Less Time You Can Hold It

Long shots (LS) and medium shots (MS) can be held for almost any length of time. Close-ups (CU and XCU), however, cannot be used for more than a few seconds.

Example: the human eye can tolerate looking at a face of a horse in a medium close-up (MCU) for a fair amount of time, even though we seldom see horses from that perspective. Inter-cutting to a close-up (CU), however, means that now we are probably seeing only a portion of the horse's face such as the mouth, nose or eye. Being that close to an animal's mouth, nose or eye is not pleasant for an extended period of time. The picture should not be held longer than :02.

Close-Ups (CU) or Extreme Close-Ups (XCU) of the Human Face Give Special problems

It is disconcerting to look at an isolated feature of a human face.

Example: Do not try to hide a person's identity in an interview by shooting only his mouth. The effect is grotesque and no one will listen to what he is saying.

Material Objects Take on a New Dimension When Perceived in an Extreme Close-Up (XCU)

Examples: a common strawberry looks like a bright red pillow. A tap or drill bit might look like a modern sculpture. They're fascinating but shouldn't be held for longer than 2 seconds and work best when edited to or from the medium close-up.

The Relationship of Pictures to One Another

Pictures are either shot sequentially or non-sequentially. Non-sequential photography is a series of different shots that are related to one another only through subject matter. Some are long-shots (LS), some are medium shots (MS) while others might be, but rarely are, close-ups. (CU). Non-sequential photography frequently uses *secondary motion*: pans, zooms and tilts.

As we said earlier, in *sequential* video each shot is a member of the same family. Think of the father as a long shot (LS), the mother as a medium shot (MS) and the children as a variety of close-ups (CU, XCU). The shots are edited together to take us *closer* to the subject, giving us *details*. Sequential video usually uses primary motion instead of secondary.

Tell TV journalism stories with sequential photography as often as possible. It is more *engaging* than non-sequential.

Example: a segment of a story about a refugee camp that is needed to go with 35-seconds of VO copy.

Non-sequential video: up from black to (1) long shot pan (LSP) to establish location. This is cut to (2) a medium shot (MS) of a mother and child. This is cut to (3) a medium shot (MS) of a group of men sitting on a hillside building a fire. This is cut to (4) a medium close-up (MCU) of two women washing clothes with buckets of water. This is cut to (5) a medium close-up (MCU) of a group of children and then a slow zoom out to a long shot that includes a stray dog. *Five different shots.* (1):09, (2):07, (3):06, (4):05, (5):08, (:35).

Sequential video: up from black to (1) a long shot (LS) to establish location that includes the mother and child. This is edited to (2) a medium close-up (MCU) of the mother and child and then two close-ups (CU), (3) one of the mother's face and (4) one of the child's. This is edited to (5) a medium shot (MS) of the two men sitting on the hillside building a fire. This is cut to (6) a close-up (CU) of their hands. This is cut to two medium close-ups (MCU) (7) (8) of their respective faces. This is cut to (9) an extreme close-up (XCU) of a bucket of water being poured into a small basin. This is cut to (10) a medium shot (MS) of the two women washing clothes with this bucket. This is cut to a close-up (CU) of (11) one of their faces. This is cut to (12) a long shot (LS) revealing the stray dog and, again, showing location. *Twelve different shots.*

(1) is :04, (2) is :03, (3) is :02, (4) is :02, (5) is :04, (6) is :02, (7) is :02, (8) is :02, (9) is :03, (10) is :04, (11) is :03, (12), is :04 (:35)

Best practice:
Shoot sequentially

Tertiary Motion: Editing

Editing, in its simplest definition, is the selection, arrangement, timing and presentation of pictures and sound to tell a story. It happens in the editing room and for many TV journalists, it's the most exciting part of the creative process. Editing creates illusion and reconstructs reality. It also guides the viewers' emotional responses.

But it doesn't *begin* in the editing room. The pictures and sounds, framing and composition should become a part of everybody's thinking the moment the story is identified.

Rules! Rules! Rules!

There are rules for editing and each one is the result of media aesthetics and common practice. The goal is to present a story that communicates a sense of experience and realism. *Avoiding distractions is the ultimate objective.*

Transitions through time and space will determine whether the presentation is harsh and noticeable or smooth and "seamless." Think of craftsmanship. Think of a carpenter whose joints in a piece of furniture are invisible. Think of a tailor or seamstress whose seams are invisible.[1]

Editing practices go though periods of fashion. As just one example, about every ten years it becomes fashionable to show the edits in an interview. Each time this practice is renewed, the editors seem to believe they are the first to do it and they claim the moral high ground by asserting that edited interviews are dishonest unless the viewer can see how and when it was cut.

The same argument is offered about standard continuity. "Rules are old-fashioned" some say. But if editing rules are "old-fashioned," so then is the novel, the opera, the poem and other storytelling forms in general.

Hard and Soft

There are basically only two ways to change pictures: hard cuts or soft cuts. *Hard cuts* are blunt, one picture to the other. Soft cuts are *dissolves* when the edges are blurred from fading one into the other.

Fundamental Rule: OOF!

In order to edit gracefully, you want to avoid jump cuts. To do this, you move the object(s) *Out Of the Frame.* OOF! They can be moved at the front end of the edit or the back end. It is not necessary to move them OOF at both ends.

Example: you have a girl walking a dog in a garden.

You want to compress time and space and move both of them from one side of the garden to the other. You have two choices: (a) have the girl and the dog leave the frame and cut to them *already* in the frame in the 2nd shot or

---

[1] Having said that, some rules can be broken once in awhile. "If a thing is wrong, but it looks right, it's right. If a thing is right, but it looks wrong, it's wrong." Frederick Shook in an e-mail to the author.

(b) keep them in the frame and have them move *into* the frame in the next shot. If you kept them inside the frame and then cut to them inside the *next* frame, the edit would be aesthetically unpleasing; clumsy and ugly because they would "jump" and the background would "jump" too.

Editing Gives Energy

The number of edits determines the degree of energy. Hard cuts give more energy than dissolves. Remember also that secondary motion photography has less energy than primary. Therefore, there is a big difference between five pictures versus twelve pictures to tell the same thirty-five seconds of a story.

Refer to the story about the refugee camp. Perhaps twelve picture changes are too many for 35 seconds of VO narration? Perhaps nine is better? Perhaps even more should be used? Throughout the world, editing tempo is culturally determined.[2]

The Best Edits Are Invisible

When edits call attention to themselves, it is distracting if only for a microsecond. The human eye is quick to perceive when something is not quite right. The human eye is also forgiving and tolerates unrealistic movement if it sees it often enough. It all depends on standards.

The National Press Photographers' Association in America encourages a high standard of editing.[3] Basically, the rule is *don't edit anything that can't happen in real life.* As one authority says: "Unless your subject is a wizard like Harry Potter, she cannot be waving to the crowds in Copenhagen one second and riding a donkey in Ecuador the next."[4]

The same principle applies to a football coach walking the sideline at a game and in the next shot being interviewed in the locker room. People do not fly through the air at the speed of light, crossing time and space.[5]

Example: we watch street musicians singing, dancing and playing instruments. Later we will interview the guitar player in a different setting. We are watching and listening to the musicians in a variety of different pictures: a long-shot (LS), a series of medium shots (MS) inter-cut with several close-ups (CU). How do we get from the musicians to the interview shot in a different setting? If we cut directly from any medium close-up (MCU) or close-up (CU) of the guitar player to his "head and shoulders" shot for the interview, we are violating logic. A good transition is a *cutaway* of the audience.

---

[2] The French cut fast; Finns cut slowly; Americans, extremely fast; Danes, moderately fast.
[3] James Townley, *The Best Editing Goes Unnoticed.*
[4] Frederick Shook in an e-mail to the author.
[5] 299,792,458 meters per second.

Overlapping Action

Example: a woman is sitting down in a chair. You edit from the LS to a MS as she is sitting down, i.e., cutting *on* the actual movement , thus making a more elegant edit. Of course, this requires shooting the action two times: once from a distance (LS) and once closer up (MS) as they do when making feature films. This is why sequential pictures are more cinematic than illustrative ones.

Cutaways

In simple language, a *cutaway* is a picture that relates to the story but does not interfere with common logic. The concept is expressed both as a verb and as a noun. We use a *cutaway* to "cut away" from the primary action. In the musician story, by cutting away to a picture of the audience and holding it for a good chunk of time, (4–5 seconds), we give an illusion of altered time and space and when we arrive at the interview, logic has been maintained.

What about interviewing the guitar player in the same setting as where we saw him performing? *Space* has not been violated, true, but *time* has. It's simply not logical that he can be interviewed at the same time that he is performing. We could move him OOF or use a dissolve but this is a missed opportunity to use another picture. A cutaway is better. The audience is only one choice for the cutaway, however. We could also cutaway to a close-up (CU) of the other musicians.

Example: the story is a profile of a doctor whose hobby is amateur theatre. We first meet her in a hospital, wearing a white laboratory coat. The story then cuts to her volunteer work as a drama coach for a children's theatre group. How do we get from the hospital to the theatre? Pictures of her full body and face that are edited with a hard cut violate reality. Not only does she fly through the air at the speed of light but she also changes her clothes. Thus, the edit has violated two rules of logic: *time* and *space*.

What should we do? To begin with, this story is different from the musicians' story because it has chapters. It's rather primitive to go from one chapter to another with a jump cut. We could use a dissolve but this is lazy and a missed opportunity for a picture and NATURAL SOUND. To edit the doctor in her white lab coat in a hospital setting to a theatre stage where she is sitting with several children, we need a *neutral* shot that relates to the story but doesn't interfere with logic, which will also advance the story. This is where NATURAL SOUND works well.

An effective transition in this story might be a close-up (CU) or medium close-up (MCU) of children sitting on a stage with an A-V sound bite of their voices as they chat, waiting for their drama coach. The doctor is not in the picture and there is no VO narration yet from the journalist. We establish the new chapter and then the story can continue.[6]

---

[6] See Chapter 2 for a more complete discussion of using natural sound as a transition between chapters.

Avoid the "Tulip Cutaway"

Many cutaways in interviews are medium close-ups (MCU) or close-ups (CU). Avoid, however, what in Denmark is called the "tulip cut." It is not wise to cut to a vase of flowers that we have never seen. It distracts and sabotages its very purpose. If the vase of flowers has been present during the interview, however, and the eye has seen it in the background, the cutaway will work. Otherwise, it's ridiculous! Why should a vase of flowers suddenly appear on the screen?

Action/Reaction

This is a good concept to remember when looking for cutaways. Whenever there is *action*, there is usually *reaction*. Performances have an audience. Accidents have observers. Sporting events have spectators. "Shoot the audience!" is a good rule of thumb.

Don't Be Lazy! Set a High Standard

You can see illogical edits every day in news programmes and documentaries. People fly across time and space at the speed of light and just for fun, we might call these edits "Harry Potter cuts." Just because they show up in TV stories, however, doesn't justify their use.

Any edit that calls attention to itself is primitive. Avoid "Harry Potter" edits. *Use a cutaway.* Use them to cover edits in interviews. Use them to maintain continuity.

But remember to shoot them! They must be planned and recorded. Otherwise, you won't have them when you need them.

> **Best practice:**
> Use cutaways

What's the Essential Difference between a Hard Cut and a Dissolve?

Before technology made it easy, overlapping images in a "dissolve" was cumbersome work. Today it requires no more effort than a few movements with a computer mouse. But why use a dissolve? Does the human eye even perceive overlapping images? Yes it does, and a dissolve communicates a change in *time* and *space*.

Use a Dissolve to Show that Time Has Passed

It is especially useful in showing a process.

Example: you want to show the making of a ceramic vase. To show it in real time would require several hours if not days. By using dissolves you can compress time and space as you go from one step to the other to the final product.

Example: you want to show the growth of a small company that started with one employee, then three, then six until today when it employs twenty-five. Using the same room, photograph the original employee alone. Then slowly add each of the others, being careful to keep everyone in his original place within the frame of the picture. Using the dissolve from one edit to the next, you can show the company's growth in a matter of seconds. The opposite effect can also be created.

Example: a school used to have 25 students. Two years ago it had twelve. Today it has only five.

Example: a company used to have ten women employees: Today it has none.

Use a Dissolve to Cover a Jump Cut in an Interview

The "twitching body" in an edited interview is an ugly edit and should be avoided. If you insist on showing where the interview was edited, use a dissolve to soften the rough edges. Hard cuts using cutaways, however, are preferable to dissolves because they have more energy. (See Chapter 9 for the five ways to mask the jump cuts when editing interviews.)

Respect Vectors

In media aesthetics, a perceivable force with a direction and magnitude is a vector.[7] If you carefully examine the various ways visual vectors operate, you are likely to find three principal types: (a) graphic vectors, (b) index vectors, and (c) motion vectors.

Graphic vectors: a vector created by lines or stationary elements that are arranged in such a way as to suggest a line. This line can be horizontal, vertical or curved. The concept is used consciously or unconsciously in creating picture composition.

Index vectors: these are created by stationary elements that guide our eyes in certain directions. The most common "stationary element" is something with a point on its end such as an arrow, a finger, or the brim of a baseball cap. Another example is two human faces in profile looking in the same direction so that their noses serve as pointing fingers.

Why do we need to pay attention to these index vectors? Because the frame of a TV screen has an invisible magnetism that "pulls" on objects and can pull them "out of the frame" if they are too close to the frame's edges. The composition of a picture will work well or not so well, depending on the framing of the index vector. A still photograph of a moving object is an index vector, by the way, not a motion vector.

---

[7] In mathematics, a vector is a physical quantity with both a magnitude and direction.

Index vectors are the reason that we want "headroom" over the top of a presenter's head in the studio. The head at the top of a body points upward and needs room to avoid the "pulling effect" from the invisible magnetism of the frame. Likewise, someone wearing a baseball cap (not backwards but the correct way for which the cap was designed) needs to be framed to allow room for the "pull" that is created by the brim.

Motion vectors: This is a vector created by an object actually moving in a specific direction. Why we need to pay attention to them is that we can sabotage our story if we lay a VO from the subject over pictures with strong motion vectors.

When Motion Vectors Distract

This is a common mistake TV journalists make when they do portraits. They ask us to pay attention to two things at the same time – but we don't! Motion vectors are too much competition for VO comments and we usually choose the pictures over the sound track.

Example: if the profile is about a boy at a boarding school for football training, we won't hear much of what he is saying about his daily life if we're hearing his VO while watching football pictures with action. If the profile is about a politician and she is talking about committee work, we won't really listen to her if we are watching her cut up vegetables and meat and start to cook a stir-fry in a wok pan. If the profile is about a karate champion and he is talking about the spiritual side of the discipline, we'll miss half of what he is saying if he's kicking, falling and grunting at the same time. Listen to this VO from a boy at a football boarding school.

> *VO: We get up early and we have chores. Sometimes we work in the kitchen. Other times, we have to clean the bathrooms. Then we have breakfast. The food is good. Really tasty! And very nutritious. In the beginning I missed junk food but now I look forward to fruit, whole grains and vegetables. Before we start to play, we have 30 minutes of warm up exercises. These are important.*

If we lay this VO over pictures of the boy playing football, chances are we won't hear very much of what he is saying. Why? Because motion vectors have energy and they demand our attention. Our brain doesn't like to pay attention to both things at the same time, and most of us would rather watch football played than hear about nutritious food. Therefore, we choose to watch the sport and we stop listening to what he is saying. Journalistically speaking, the information is wasted.

Avoid using pictures that compete with the VO for the viewer's attention. Instead, let the pictures breathe! Let the NATURAL SOUND tell part of the story. Let the viewer experience what is going on.

Best practice:
Pay attention to motion vectors

When Motion Vectors Allow the Viewer to Experience the Story

Motion vectors work well, however, if the subject of the VO is the same subject as that the pictures communicate. The use of motion vectors works to advance the story when we, as viewers, get to *experience* what the VO is expressing.

Positive example: VO: I love this school because I love playing football! I'm learning a lot about strategy and the mental side of the game. (*football game walla :10 while we watch the boys play.*) VO: I'm also learning a lot about teamwork and how to trust my colleagues. (*football walla :08 while we watch interaction with the other players.*)

Positive example: VO: I was afraid of my new job at first. Just after I was elected I hated committee work. I was afraid that people wouldn't like my ideas. (*fly-on-the-wall :10 while we listen to the new politician present a report using PowerPoint or a flip chart.*) VO: Now it's different. I feel more confident.

Positive example: VO: Karate like other martial arts requires meditation. I need to sit perfectly still and quiet myself. (*room tone :10 while we feel his quietness*)

VO: I get a lot of energy from this.

The Z Axis

No matter if they are primary or secondary, most pictures have movement that is either horizontal or vertical. Movement *towards* the viewer, however, is on the Z axis. This is an index and motion vector that points or moves toward or away from the camera.

Example: a fast train that comes towards us, giving the viewer the sensation of moving directly into the lens.

Shooting a scene "on the Z axis" is the most effective way *to buy screen time.* Real-time or manipulated time can be used by shooting the action with the zoom lens. In this way you can keep the moving object in the same place by zooming out as they come closer.

Tempo Is Determined by Editing VO First

Tempo is best determined by the *rhythm* of the voice-over narration (VO) when each edit is cut on words that are punched with extra energy from the journalist's voice. We call these pulse points. The reporter's tempo, therefore, determines the style and feeling of the story.

In order to make picture changes an *organic* part of the story, they must be edited *to* the VO narration. Unless the VO is recorded first, the pictures cannot be edited with rhythm.

This is evident when you hear a VO narration that was recorded after the pictures were edited because there *are* no pulse points. The pictures come in at *random*. Hence, some VO narration is spoken very rapidly with few picture changes while others are spoken slowly with many picture changes. Using an analogy: when the pictures are edited first, they often dance the tango while the VO narration dances a waltz or a polka. The best editing happens when they are both dancing the same dance!

Edit with Rhythm

When we edit pictures with music, we cut *to* the music track. We do not lay down the pictures first because we want the edits to correspond to the *rhythm* of the music. The same principle applies to songs. Singing uses words but the pictures are edited *to* the words in order to maintain the rhythm.

Why not with the spoken word? Of all the techniques that have been borrowed in Europe from North America, editing *to* the VO narration is the one that is seldom adopted. This is puzzling to consultants and guest teachers who cannot understand the fierce resistance. There is no logical reason. The most common response is a simple: "that's not the way we do it here."

Consider, however, the benefits of such a technique. Not all VO narration is read in similar ways because the journalist needs to use a voice and inflection that suits the particular story. When the VO narration is edited first, the pictures can be edited *precisely* where the voice commands it. Using these pulse points is one way to enhance fascination in information-based stories.

It is technically possible to edit on pulse points when the pictures are put in first but it requires the journalist to read the copy several times before every pulse point hits the target.

Editing the VO narration first, therefore, can save valuable time and much frustration. The journalist has control of the story and is no longer a "hostage" to the tempo of the pictures. In this way, pauses for A-V bites can be planned and prepared for.

Example: consider the following copy to see where the pulse points are in different places.

1. **A-V tease:** *rushing river :05.*
    VO: It was **here** on this bridge that the brakes failed on the school bus *(Ssshhhhhhh! :03 traffic whizzing by)*. VO: The driver lost control and tried to **stop** the vehicle by turning the wheels into the wall. Several **children** fell against the seats and windows and many of them are in hospital tonight with injuries. *("Move it! Move it! yells the driver of an emergency vehicle as a crane, buuuuuurah :03 lifts the bus from the wall)*. VO: **No one** was killed. The driver survived with cuts to his forehead **and** a wounded reputation.

2. **A-V tease:** *rushing river :05.*
    VO: It was here – on **this** bridge that the brakes failed on the school bus." *(Ssshhhhhhh! :03 Traffic whizzing by)*. VO: The driver lost control and tried to stop the vehicle by turning the **wheels** into the wall. Several children fell against the seats and windows and many of them are in hospital tonight with **injuries.** *("Move it! Move it! yells the driver of an emergency vehicle as a crane, buuuuuurah :03 lifts the bus from the wall)*. VO: No one was **killed.** The driver survived with cuts to his **forehead** and a wounded reputation."

> **Best practice:**
> Treat the spoken voice as a musical instrument

When Interviews Are Used as VO

Edited segments from interviews are called *syncs* because they are synchronised sound from a person's lips.

If an edited segment from an interview is lengthy (20–45 seconds) it is a common practice to edit it as VO. If pictures are cut on the *rhythm* of the spoken words, the result is aesthetically satisfying. If pictures are cut at random, it lacks harmony and is less pleasing to the eye and ear.

Don't Step on the Natural Sound Bites

The value of NATURAL SOUND is that it takes the viewers into the story and allows them to experience the event. If you don't *stop talking* for 2–3 seconds however, we won't hear it. We call this stepping on your bite. If the VO continues over the top of the NATURAL SOUND, 75% of its power is lost!

> **Best practice:**
> Stop talking!

When Rhythm Doesn't Matter

Sports stories often involve "play-by-play" narration. Pictures first and then the VO. No pulse points. Therefore, no rhythm. In addition, laying the voice track *over* pictures works well when the material is lyrical. Examples are any nature story about animals, a safari tour or a travel documentary. Editing pictures first also works well for educational and historical documentaries.

Consider the National Geographic film, *March of the Penguins* that won the 2006 Academy Award for best feature documentary. This outstanding example of picture-sound storytelling about penguins at the South Pole astounded audiences with its story of love and survival. Working with pictures first and then adding the VO was the only way to produce it.

> **Best practice:**
> Edit pictures first when rhythm doesn't matter

Color or Black/White

It is not uncommon to relish old black and white movies. The American 1942 classic, *Casablanca* is an example as well as Vittorio De Sica's 1949 *The Bicycle Thief*. These films are unforgettable not just because of their outstanding photography but precisely because there is no colour.

We like black and white movies because they are emotional and we like emotions because they make us feel alive. How does this happen? Photography with normally saturated colours contains more *information* than black and white photography and it is the degree of information that affects perception. When images are low-definition, we must "fill in" the "missing parts" mentally. When we do this, we participate at a higher level in the perception of the event and it is the *participation* that makes it an emotional experience.

This is a basic principle of applied media aesthetics and it has consequences. In other words, it means something when the colour is removed. TV journalists can easily manipulate the viewer's perception by removing colour.

Best practice:
Don't remove colour without a reason

Example: a story is about a senior citizens' home where most of the residents are lonely. Interviews reveal how infrequently their grown children visit them and the pictures show them alone in their rooms. If the colour is taken out of the pictures, the story is perceived on a more emotional level than when it is seen in colour. It is debatable whether it is ethical in journalism to manipulate the viewer's perception and perhaps, in the final analysis, it is a question of taste.

In the meantime, the producers of commercials certainly understand this principle and this is why there is an accelerated use of black and white in advertising. Steven Spielberg probably had this aesthetic principle in mind when he made *Schindler's List* in black and white. It must have also been in the minds of the Danish Red Cross when they made their 2006 public service announcement with Crown Prince Frederik about starvation in Africa. Black and white only. No colour.

Understanding the aesthetic principles of colour gives the TV photographer and journalist many options. One could purposely under expose pictures to give them lower definition or remove the colour altogether. By using filters and gels, one could emphasise warm or cold colours to give a specific feeling. One could use shadows to accentuate the height or width of objects.

More good advice:
When recording a shot, it is recommended that you hold it for a minimum of 15–20 seconds. This gives you room to edit.

4 Deciding the Story's Treatment

Every democratic culture that supports a free press has basically two kinds of journalism: hard and soft. These adjectives do not really describe the true nature of these types, however, because *hard* suggests "important" and *soft* suggests "unimportant" or "frivolous." The two terms are too limiting and misleading. If we look deeper into the two categories, we can see how some soft stories can be highly significant with considerable substance.

Whether hard or soft, a story needs a plan for how it will be told. This is called a treatment.

Information-based stories: news bulletins answer the fundamental questions *what, when, where* and *who*. Current affairs stories go deeper and one step further by answering *why*. Both are current. Both are time-locked. Both are hard news.

Features are not time-locked stories. They usually describe ordinary people doing extraordinary things or extraordinary people doing ordinary things. Print journalists were the first to call them "human interest" stories and conventionally, they are considered soft stories. Unlike hard news that is often unpleasant, features are usually cheerful, pleasant and attractive. (*"I wouldn't mind seeing that again!"*) Features charm us and make us feel good by involving us, engaging our emotions and telling us something about ourselves.

Reporting: Top Down, Outside Looking In

Traditionally speaking, both types – hard and soft – are *top down* or told from "outside looking in." The journalist *reports* to the viewer and uses segments from interviews to document claims or assertions.

In **information-based stories**, the edited segments from interviews are relatively short (10–20 seconds) as either support (facts) or colour (opinions). The reporter's participation is approximately 70% of the story, reporting through a VO, using articulate pictures and NATURAL SOUND. The story is constructed in layers and moves ahead in one direction. Often a person will *illustrate* the issue and this is called a "case study."

Some information-based stories are "sexy" meaning they have instant audience appeal. At the other extreme are BBI stories, "boring but important."

In **features**, the edited segments from interviews are often longer (25–50 seconds) and many are used as voice-overs. The participation of the journalist varies from 70% to 50% to as little as 10%. The story has "chapters" but can zig-zag, interlacing elements in a creative manner. If there is a "case study," the person serves as an *illustration*.

Fascination. DOI: 10.1016/B978-0-12-416037-8.00004-3

In Anglo-American broadcasting organisations, the top down journalist is frequently on camera: walking and talking; serving as a cutaway to mask an interview edit; asking an on-camera question; or talking directly into the lens in a stand-up (called piece-to-camera in the United Kingdom).

Storytelling Through People Stories: Eye Level, Inside Looking Out

Another type of story that falls in neither category – hard or soft – abandons reporting in favour of *storytelling*. The stories are told from eye level or "inside looking out." Serious topics are told *through people* – not the reporter – using interviews from a case study to define the issues. In this way, the case study is the *focus* of the story, not merely an illustration. The journalist is seldom if ever seen but there are usually voice-overs (VOs) to link segments.

Top down stories are relatively objective. Eye level stories are relatively subjective. Top down stories are relatively intellectual. Eye level stories are relatively emotional.

Significant Vision

Journalism stories are no different from novels, theatre plays, films, operas, painting, symphonies or other forms of the public arts. They have to be relevant to human life and reflect our common humanity. The degree of complexity varies with the target audience and in mass communication we are expected to "connect" with as many people as we can. Any story worth telling has *significant vision.*

- A problem to be solved
- A challenge to be met
- An obstacle to be overcome
- A threat to be handled
- A decision or choice to be made
- A pressure to be relieved
- A tension to be eased
- A victory to be celebrated
- A kindness to be acknowledged

Choosing the Story's Treatment

- Consider the TOPIC.
- What are the different ANGLES the topic can have?
- Which angle will leave the viewer the most INFORMED?
- How much INFORMATION is necessary to inform?
- Is the story top down or eye level?
- Top down feature or a "people story?"
- What NATURAL SOUND can be used to maximise fascination?

How Many Minutes Should the Story Be?

This is one of the most important questions in the treatment phase. In order to *develop* a story, the journalist needs to have a block of *time*. Short stories can be 2:30 and in some cases, 4:00 or 6:00 or maybe even 8:00. If they are longer than this, they start to fall into the category of a mini-documentary.

Most news editors might feel that today's viewer lacks the patience for long stories in an ordinary news broadcast. This is determined by national culture and will be different in every TV industry. If a developed story is too long for a regular newscast, however, there might be other informative programmes on the station where it can be aired.

Some stories deserve an entire documentary at 30:00 or one hour. We've all seen documentaries, however, that would have been better as an 8:00–12:00 segment in a magazine programme. Ultimately, this is an editorial decision.

Is It a Picture Story?

Some stories are easily "good television" because they are inherently visual: a train wreck. A flood. A famine. Not always pretty pictures, but strong visuals. Not all visual stories are catastrophes, of course. Here is a list of ordinary stories that are easily visual.

- Why Scandinavia is the best places for mothers
- How European café society is coping with the new non-smoking regulations
- New policies for paternal-leave and infant care
- The "brain drain" of professionals from Estonia, Poland, Lithuania and Latvia to the Nordic nations
- Why SUV vehicles are becoming more popular even in environmentally-sensitive cultures

BBIs

When stories are not inherently visual but the topic is important, we might call them: BBIs, *boring but important*. Ninety-nine percent of BBI stories are information-based.

These stories need constructed pictures, often from archives, and a string of experts to explain the issues. Since the mid-90s, it has become fashionable in some broadcast cultures to renounce BBIs and some TV journalists refuse to produce them. This is because they often lack engagement and are indeed, boring!

BBI is not an excuse to abandon the topic. Instead, they should be perceived as a challenge. BBIs need careful attention to NATURAL SOUND and the best pictures possible to accompany the VO. Interview segments from experts must be kept short and a case study can make a world of difference by showing us the human side of the issue. Consider these non-visual stories but important stories:

- Toxic chemicals in the home
- The politics of solar energy
- The high cost of "high tech"
- New union regulations
- Tax reform
- Solid waste and refuse management

5 Top Down Features

In top down feature stories, the journalist takes responsibility for the story but uses segments from interviews to tell major parts of it. *The proportion of VO to SYNCS varies.* The interviews either *support* asserted claims or add *colour* by giving opinions. Case studies are merely *illustrations* but not the focus.

In some stories, the personality of the journalist is featured. In others, the journalist is relatively invisible. The extent to which the journalist appears in the story is culturally determined.

The best characteristic of a feature story is that it communicates a sense of *experience*.

Example: dense fog at the airport detains Christmas travellers. An information-based story would show the fog, the stranded airplanes and frustrated passengers while the journalist gives the meteorological facts in a VO. A feature tells the same story through people's individual experiences. How?

The photographer shoots *what is happening* through fly-on-the-wall and the journalist writes *to* the pictures, filling in the gaps with appropriate commentary but allowing the pictures and their NATURAL SOUND to tell the story of impatience and frustration.

What is it like to spend Christmas at an airport? *Things happen* in such a situation: a toddler chooses this time to start walking; a couple decides to get engaged; a woman finishes knitting a sweater for her first grandchild; a writer finishes his novel on his laptop computer. Waiting at an airport can be an opportunity for "slice of life" stories.

Because features are not dominated by facts, they don't necessarily need a context. Neither do they require a summary at the end and can therefore finish with a pithy statement from one of the main characters.

Feature stories often use music, an element that tends to trivialise an information-based story. Choosing the right music is part of the creative process. Many features have been sabotaged by the wrong melodies, inappropriate rhythms or using a cut with lyrics under a VO.

A sub-category of the **feature** is the ***news feature***. This is not time-locked but for the sake of clarity, it is produced like an information-based story.

Guidelines for producing top down features:

- You have a topic and you go out and shoot. Now you must have a story to tell using the pictures and NATURAL SOUND.
- You need a MESSAGE in your story. It can't just be a "collection of impressions." Find an angle with significant vision and then try writing to your pictures. Ask yourself: *"What do the pictures make me say?"*

Fascination. DOI: 10.1016/B978-0-12-416037-8.00005-5

- Give your story structure. Break it down into chapters. Information-based stories must move forward in one direction. In features you can "zig-zag" if it helps to make it engaging.
- If you have good interviews, allow them to tell the story. Show their faces or use segments of the SYNCS as a VO with pictures.

Be careful! Make sure the pictures are in harmony with what is being said in the VO. If the pictures compete for the viewer's attention, the information in the VO might not be perceived. (see the sections on vectors in Chapter 3).

- Link each section of the story with a VO from you but keep it at a minimum, if you are not needed to tell the story.
- Use NATURAL SOUND as much as possible. This allows the viewer to *experience* what's going on. Be careful not to step on A-V bites with SYNCS and VOs. Interrupt the spoken language. Let the sounds breathe!

Example 1: **African dance is popular in Denmark**. The hobby is growing as more and more Danes find emotional therapy in this highly rhythmic dance form. Ordinary Danes from ordinary middle class lifestyles tell in VOs how it feels to move their bodies to drums. Music is dominant. A VO from a journalist links the sections and gives context.

Fade up from black: a slow pan over a typical Danish countryside with wind in the trees. **A-V tease: *Shoooo! :04*.** Fade up music: ***Boom… boom boom! :04***. Cut to the interior of a Danish country cottage and reveal the source of the music: an African man is sitting in a Danish living room playing a drum. ***Boom boom boom! :06***. A small boy dances next to him. Cut away to his Danish mother. These are his parents. They have brought African dance to this Danish community.

Now a second woman is next to the boy and she dances and shakes a small percussion instrument. ***Shake shake! :04***. VO: We started dancing after I met my husband on an anthropology dig in Kenya. Eventually we came home to Denmark. ***Shake shake! Boom boom! Shake! Shake! Shake! Boom boom!:06***. VO: He introduced us to African dance. Several of our friends started coming around and soon we had a club. ***Boom boom! Shake! Boom!:04***. SYNC: *"We love it! It's better than playing sports! We can't get enough of it!"* ***Boom boom boom!:03***.

Dissolve: one drum becomes several. ***BOOM d' boom! BOOM d' boom boom! :06***. CU of hands on drum. Wide shot: three musicians in an auditorium. In front of them are two rows of Scandinavian women dancing and clapping their hands. VO: I started dancing two years ago. ***Clap! Clap! Clap clap clap! :06***. VO: I feel so much better after I dance for an hour. ***Clap clap! Clap clap clap! :04***. SYNC: *"I can't begin to express it really. It just makes me feel so happy!"*

The viewer's reaction: "That was fun! I'd like to see it again!"

Example 2: **Danish folk high schools are unusual schools where you don't get grades**. A Spanish journalist visits one of these traditional schools where we meet young Danes who are between secondary and university level education. The students spend six months learning new things for which they'll not be given grades. It's learning for learning's sake. The *folkehøjskole* also teaches "community," an important value in Danish democracy. The story is told 80% through SYNCS and interview VOs.

Fade up from black. MCU of clay and hands on a spinning ceramics wheel. **A-V tease:** *Whirrrl! Whirrrl! :02*. VO: I always wanted to learn how to throw a pot but this is my first opportunity. Cut to MCU of Rasmus at the wheel. *Whirrrl! Whirrl! :02*. SYNC: *"I've never felt artistic before but here nobody cares if you're really good or not."* *Whirrrrrrrrrrrrl! :04*. Cut to CU of clay thrown onto a table. *Plop! :01*. VO: Here we can try out new things. L cut to plucked guitar strings: *Boing boing!* Cut to wide shot of a small music band. Rasmus is playing the electric bass. The students begin to play. *Music up full :08*. Music under. VO: This is something else I've always wanted to do. I was afraid before to even try. *Music up full :05*. VO: I'm not sure what we sound like but it's fun!

The viewer's reaction: "Wow! That's really cool! I wish we had something like that in our country!"

Example 3: Camp Fjordmark is a summer camp for overweight children where they learn self-esteem and healthy eating habits. They also learn to trust adults and to make friends. We meet "Niels," "Anna" and "Sarah" and see how they spend their time.

Fade up from black: **A-V tease:** *MCU of a hand cutting vegetables. Chop! chop, chop! :03*. Cut to wide shot then MCU of various salads in a line of bowls. L-cut to *room walla :02* and a wide shot of children eating in a dining hall. Inter-cut to MCU of over-weight Niels (age 11) and a teacher. **Fly-on-the-wall A-V bite:** *"That was a good painting you made, Niels. Really nice! I'd like to hang it on the wall of my office."* Cut to CU of Niels. He smiles. Cut to CU of teacher. **Fly-on-the-wall A-V bite continues:** *"It's easier for you to get up in the morning now, right? I like it when you come to class on time. Don't you?"*

L cut *music :04*. Cut to CU of a girl's feet in an exercise class. Cut to MS of over-weight Anna (age 10) in a group. VO: Listen up! I want to start from the beginning but only the left side of the room this time. OK? Got it? Long shots of Anna and two friends as they begin to move to the music. Sequential shots. *Music under :09*. VO: I love it here! I never want to go home. At my regular school I don't have any friends but here....that's Sarah. She's my best friend! We met here at Camp Fjordmark. *Music up full :04*. The girls move to the music. Cross fade music to L cut of *brush, brush, brush! :03*.

Cut to: CU toothpaste tube. Cut to wide shot of over-weight Sarah and over-weight Anna brushing their teeth. *Brush, brush, brush! :03*. CU Anna. Sarah's voice in a VO: Anna is my best friend. I wish she went to my regular school. **Fly-on-the-wall A-V bites:** *"Why do you keep using my toothpaste? Haven't you got any of your own?" "Look who's talking! You used mine all last summer!"* L-cut of *room wallah :04*. CU of sleeping bags. Cut to a wide shot of the dormitory where the girls sleep. Cut to MCU of Anna and Sarah crawling into their sleeping bags. **Fly-on-the-wall A-V bite:** *"Don't keep me awake tonight, OK? I don't want any more of your dumb jokes!"* (Laughter).

CU of foot kicking soccer ball. *Whoooosh!* Cut to MCU of a teacher, watching from the sidelines. SYNC: *"It's really quite amazing how much they change during a summer."* Cut to: action play with sound up full: *sports field wallah :06*. SYNC: *"When they get here they're often very lonely. Fat kids get teased a lot in school but here with others like themselves, they relax and start to make friends."*

The viewer's reaction: "These summer camps are wonderful! What a good idea!"

News features are "soft" stories that use the strict model for information-based stories, usually because the material is complex with many facts.

Example: the Jewish cemetery in Aarhus has a gravestone for a man from Vilnius in Lithuania. Who was he? How did he end up in Denmark? The man has been deceased for 100 years and there are no witnesses to his life. Using a local historian, a Lithuanian journalist reconstructs his history with documents, archive pictures and beautiful photography of the cemetery. The story unfolds with a tease, context, development and wrap.

Here NATURAL SOUND is used to raise the level of engagement. At the cemetery we hear the sounds of wind in the trees (*whooooo :03*) and autumn leaves blowing across the paths. *(crinkle crinkle :04)*. Footsteps *(wamp wamp wamp! :04)* on the path and then the leaves (*crunch…. crunch…. crunch :05*). Someone opens a gate *(errrrrr :02)*. In the archive, there are the sounds of drawers being opened and closed, pages being turned and *squeak!* as a chair is moved to a table. Lithuanian folk music is used to create nostalgia under old photographs.

Good advice:

Before you start to record, *label your tape*: name, date, project and number. Many recorded tapes have been lost because they were not labeled. *An unlabeled tape is an accident waiting to happen.*

6 Top Down Information Stories

> **Information:**
> Facts, facts and more facts! experts, critics, statistics.

Some journalists have gone to journalism school. Others have learned on the job. Whatever their educational background, journalists are trained *to manage information*.

They do this by conducting research, interviewing, verifying sources and then explaining issues to the public. Traditional journalists report stories and they're called reporters.

Many traditional journalists, especially those from the print medium, tend to believe that information alone is the breath that gives life to the profession. *Facts! Information! Analysis!* Everything else is relatively unimportant.

What About Identification and Fascination?

Information-based stories can establish identification by using case studies as *illustrations* of the issue. They can enhance fascination by using the medium to its best potential. Unless there are articulate pictures and a generous use of NATURAL SOUND, the viewer remains psychologically detached and the emotional part of communication is lost.

News bulletins are information-based but they're not really stories. News bulletins are headlines with a few details.

Observe the essential differences between news bulletins and a developed story.

News	Current Affairs
:30, 1:20, 1:45	2:45, 4:00, 7:00, 30:00
FACTS: who? what? when? where?	why? so what?
	CONTEXT: summarises who, what, when, where
now! event driven	recently but not today
objective; balanced	fair but not necessarily objective; challenges our emotions; makes us care!
limited analysis	analytical: makes us think!
usual cast of characters	new characters
shallow	layered
predictable	requires framing from new angles

Fascination. DOI: 10.1016/B978-0-12-416037-8.00006-7

The Storytelling Model

We borrow this storytelling model from the traditional three act structure found in theatre. The middle part of a story in which the information is developed uses a structure of several sub-acts, including a point of no return and often, though not always, a climax. If we were to diagram it, it would look like this:

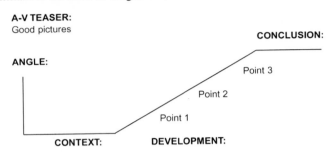

Audio-video teaser: :02-:03 NATURAL SOUND with pictures followed by 1–2 clear sentences that give the *angle* of the story.

Context: all stories require background information to give a context to the story. Without this, the details do not make sense. Information-based stories work best when the context immediately follows the angle.

Development: to keep the angle sharp, tell the story through two to three points that are directly related to the angle and subordinate to it. (Think of the angle as an umbrella). Each point is a claim or an assertion that you need to prove. The proof comes from documentation that is edited segments from interviews. Organise the points to follow the principles of drama. Save the most dramatic point until last.

Wrap or conclusion: This is a summary of the story, reminding the viewer of the "big picture;" the essential issues plus new information.

The Triple T Formula

Developed stories have structure and move from the general to the specific and back to the general. This formula is deductive–inductive–deductive and corresponds to the three acts. In print journalism, we often think of an inverted pyramid. In television information-based stories, think of a diamond.

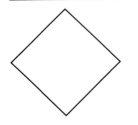

T1-General
The angle is the "umbrella" concept.

T2-Specific
begins with a brief context of the story and then develops through separate points. Each is a claim that is documented by short segments of interview.

T3-General
A summary and perspective.

At the top is the general information: *tell me what you want to tell me.* In the broad middle section are the specifics: *so tell me!* You begin with the context and then move through points 1, 2 and 3. At the bottom of the diamond you return to the general again: *tell me what you told me.* Make a summary. Add new information if it is relevant and does not depart from the angle.

Another way to describe this model is to call it a "package." The story is self-contained and does not require the studio presenter to give 15% of the story.

We superimpose the Triple T formula on the story model:

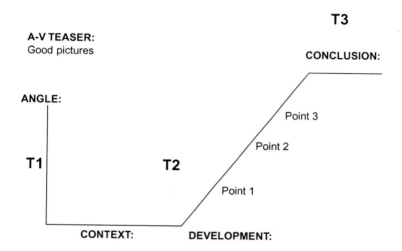

T1: Finding the Angle (General)

Tell me what you want to tell me.

The angle of the story is not the topic of the story.

Topics are subjects. But not all subjects are worthy of development beyond news bulletin headlines. Does the topic have significant vision? If yes, find an angle. Angles give the topic *focus.*

How do we find an angle? Look for the conflict!

- A problem to be solved
- A challenge to be met
- An obstacle to be overcome
- A threat to be handled
- A decision or choice to be made
- A pressure to be relieved
- A tension to be eased
- A victory to be celebrated
- A kindness to be acknowledged

EXAMPLE TOPIC: the Danish royal family in the twenty-first century. OK. So what do you want to say about it? Here are two possible angles:

- Angle 1: it costs Danish taxpayers 10 million euros a year to support this concept of inherited privilege. What do they get for their money? *(A pressure to be relieved)*
- Angle 2: It is not appropriate for a modern democracy to maintain a family whose members have no political rights and no freedom of religion. *(A problem to be solved.) (A tension to be eased.)*

EXAMPLE TOPIC: Danish children are eating 16 kilos of sweets a year!
There are three possible angles to this topic.

- Angle 1: eating sweets in Denmark has tripled in 25 years with serious health consequences. *(An obstacle to be overcome.)*
- Angle 2: European children are becoming overweight in general, but why are Danish kids becoming less so? *(A problem to be solved.)*
- Angle 3: Danish health camps for kids with special problems help those who are overweight. *(A pressure to be relieved.)*

EXAMPLE TOPIC: compared to many modern nations, motherhood is best in Scandinavia.

- Angle 1: the welfare state is good for mothers and children. *(A problem to be solved.)*
- Angle 2: "failed states" need to copy the Scandinavian model. *(A problem to be solved.)*
- Angle 3: why can't the USA be kinder to mothers? *(A problem to be solved.)*

Producing the Angle

Example one: the Danish royal family is Denmark's biggest public relations agency.
A-V tease: *crowd walla :04. Amalienborg Castle in Copenhagen. Crown Prince Frederik and Princess Mary stand on the balcony waving to a large crowd.*
VO: They cost ten million Euros a year but most Danes think they're worth it! *Crowd walla :03.* VO: It's an old fashioned institution. But modern PR in a globalised economy!
Example two: eating sweets in DK has tripled in 25 year with serious consequences for health.
A-V tease: *Shooooup! :04. CU of sweets sliding into a paper bag from a tall plastic dispenser.*
VO: Sixteen kilos a year! This is how much sweets Danish children eat. The consequences for their health are serious.
Example three: Sweden and Denmark rank one and two in a world survey about society's support for mothers.
A-V tease: *fly-on-the-wall of a 2 year old girl on her mother's lap. Look, Katarina! See grandpa there! Wave Katarina! Wave to grandpa! :05.*
VO: Motherhood. It's as old as human history but here in Scandinavia, they've never had it so good. In fact, they have it best in the world!

How Does Research Affect Your Angle?

Competent journalists know that gathering information can move them away from their original angle onto a new one. Don't force an angle. Make sure it fits with your research.

Example: the story is about increased jail sentences for rapists in Denmark. The context of the story is increased rape and the over-representation of Muslims among the perpetrators. This statement is verifiable from statistics. Yet the story begins to change when the journalists discover that experts are unwilling to cooperate and comment on the statistics.

Now the angle of the story has shifted to the "gap of silence." Why won't people talk? Political correctness? Or is it the unwillingness of politicians to admit that Danish integration policies have failed? Research gives the story an entirely different focus.

Why We Don't Bury the Angle

The Triple T formula clearly indicates that we tell the audience *immediately* what the story is about. Some beginner TV students often ask why the focus must be so obvious. Why can't we bury the focus and surprise the viewer?

The answer is simple: *we don't have the time to make people guess what we want to tell them.* Time in television is a luxury. Only in long stories such as the documentary can we, perhaps, bury our focus and make people wait.

Using a Case Study

Using a real person to *illustrate* the issue is a good practice, providing you have time to find one. Indeed, many stories definitely work best if you can illustrate your claims through a real person's experience.

There are two things to consider, however: (1) make sure the person is a legitimate case. Journalists are often so eager to use a case study, they manipulate their source into a position that is not truly representative. (2) Make sure that you tie up loose ends and tell the viewer what happened to your case study. Often, we never hear about them again.

Example: the story is about fishing quotas and the European Union.

A-V tease: *boat walla: 04. A small fishing boat with two men onboard. We hear sea gulls (Cah cah! Cah) and the boat's engine and maybe some conversation from the fishermen.*

VO: Lars Nielsen is worried. His family has been fishermen for five centuries but now his livelihood is in trouble.

instead of:

VO: Fishermen take too many fish from the Atlantic, says the European Union. Now new quotas are planned.

T2: Context and Development (Specific)

This is where the information is. Without this section, the story is only headlines with a few random details. The first part of this section is the background. This gives a *context* to the story and explains why you are bothering to tell it in the first place.

What follows is the section in which different points illuminate the issue. Sharply angled stories are preferable because the viewer learns more when the story goes deeper instead of wider. All claims – or asserted statements – are *documented* by short sound bites edited from interviews. The documentation serves as *evidence*. It is, therefore, critically important that interview sound bites *always follow* VO and never precede it.

Story Example: Overweight children

Angle 1: eating sweets in DK has tripled in 25 years with serious consequences for health.

CONTEXT: VO: Modern families have more money to spend and today's children expect "Saturday sweets" every weekend. **A-V bite***: hands grabbing sweets in a bowl. Rattle rattle! :03.* Their parents and grandparents ate sweets only on special holidays, about two to three times a year. In 1980, Danish kids ate only five kilos of sweets per year. *(Chewing sound :02)*. Today, it's sixteen! *(Candy falling from dispenser :03)*

DEVELOPMENT: health consequences

point 1: overweight
point 2: tooth decay; bad gums
point 3: rise in type 2 diabetes.

Consider the other angles this story can have and how it affects both the context and development of the story.

Angle 2: many European children are overweight but why are Danish kids less overweight than others?

CONTEXT: VO: Childhood has changed. Historically, kids ran around a lot and played games. *(Kids yelling while playing :02)* Now their games are on a video screen and they sit for hours *(bonk bonk! :03)* and hours. In addition, children don't walk as much, nor ride their bicycles as far. *(Car horn, honk :01)!* Instead, their parents drive them.

DEVELOPMENT: compared to the British, Danish children are less overweight.

point 1: nutrition is taught in school
point 2: Danish kids ride bicycles more than British
point 3: the Danes have health camps

Angle 3: special health camps for kids with special problems help those who are overweight.

CONTEXT: VO: The Danish welfare state is practical. If there's a problem, they find a solution. *(Telephone rings Riiiing! :02.* The Health Ministry gives out funds for special programmes, including summer camps. That means Danish children get the help they need for a wide variety of problems. *(kids talking :03)*. The first camp for overweight kids was inspired by a postman.

DEVELOPMENT: The types of camps

point 1: camp A for overweight kids
point 2: camp B attention deficit disorder
point 3: camp C behaviour problems

Now we'll write the story out in a conventional A-V script format. Audio is on the right side. Video is on the left. SOT means "sound-on-tape."

Pay attention to the documentation. If time and length of story are critical, documentation is optional for angle and context. They are absolutely necessary, however, for the claims or points in the development. If the story can take more time, documenting the angle with a short *colour* bite enhances it.

Video	Audio
Up from black: **AV tease: *Shooooup (sweets fall through a plastic dispenser into a paper bag)***	SOT
ANGLE:	VO: Sixteen kilos a year! This is how much sweets Danish children eat with serious consequences to their health. SYNCS: (2–3 children buying Saturday sweets)
CONTEXT: **AV tease: *CU hand taking sweets from a bowl. (Rattle, rattle!)***	SOT VO: Modern families have more money to spend and today's children expect candy every Saturday. Twenty-five years ago, they ate sweets only on special holidays. In 1980, they ate only 5 kilos of sweets the whole year. That's more than a triple increase. On top of that, children don't get as much exercise today. Boys in particular sit for hours playing video games. Some girls have stopped riding bicycles.
DEVELOPMENT: Point 1: overweight **AV tease to point 1:** ***CU of feet on a scale.*** ***The child steps off and we hear the scale re-adjust.***	SOT
	VO: Being overweight is the most common consequence. Authorities say that 20% of Danish children under twelve weigh far more than they should. SYNC: (doctor :10) VO: And if they don't lose this weight by puberty, it may be too late. SYNC: (doctor :09)

(*Continued*)

(Continued)

Video	Audio
Point 2: cavities in teeth **AV tease to point 2:** *Dentist drill in a child's mouth* *Bizzzzzzzzz!*	SOT VO: No one likes to get fillings in their teeth but this is how some children are paying for their sugar habit. It's no fun! SYNC: (child :10) SYNC: (dentist :15)
Point 3: increase in type-2 diabetes **AV tease to point 3:** *CU child's arm with* **blood pressure gauge.** *(Pump pump!* *Release!)*	SOT VO: Type 2 diabetes is on the rise and many authorities think it's directly related to diet. Both children and adults eat poorly compared to their grandparents. They have more money today but they spend it on unhealthy fast food. *Sound bite:sausage street vendor.* *("Something to drink?" "Yeah, gimme a* *Coke!")* VO: Too much fat! Too much sugar! Is there anything that can be done? SYNC: (doctor or nutritionist :14)
AV tease to conclusion: *More sweets falling through the plastic* *dispenser. Shoooop! Plop!*	SOT Stand-up: All children like sweets. This has been true forever and in all cultures. It's different today, however, because children and their families have more money to spend and they spend it unwisely. Too many sweets on Saturday. Too much sugar in their lifestyles. Now the Danes want to launch a campaign to change attitudes. Their finely tuned welfare state can't tolerate health problems that could be prevented. In Denmark, I'm Sander van Zoot.
AV tag: *(same as above, repeated 3 times)* *Shooop plop, Shoop plop! Shoop plop!*	SOT

Fleshing Out the Model with Specific Points that Give the Details

Story example 1: hundreds of unemployed teachers receive unemployment insurance while they wait to be called as substitutes.

T-1: Angle: unemployed teachers do not get called for substitute teaching jobs because student-teachers are hired in their place.

T-2: Context: statistics that show an increase of this practice over the last ten years.

T2: Development:

point 1: Unemployed teachers are unreliable

point 2: Student teachers are paid less

point 3: Student teachers are smarter!

Step by Step

T1: up from black, **A-V tease:** *fly-on-the-wall "Get out your science books and turn to page 12." (:04.) A young looking teacher stands in front of a classroom of children.* VO: Student teachers work as substitutes. This is wrong, the union says because unemployed teachers should be hired first.

(The viewer says: *Oh yeah? What's this all about? Give me the details!*)

T2: A-V transition to the context: *school yard walla :02-:03.* Kids kick balls and play. VO: Since 1956, the teacher's union has given a list of unemployed teachers to schools so they can hire them as substitutes. The Hampton School District, however, is not playing by the rules the union says. This is wrong since over 300 teachers are unemployed in the district. In 1990, 32 teachers were called. In 2000, only 22. In 2004, 12. Today it is less than 5 in a school year. What's going on?

T2 continued: **A-V transition** to point 1. *Riiiing! Riiiing! Sounds of telephone :02-:03. Fly-on-the-wall: "Unemployment office! How can I help you?"* VO: Apparently, there is a large misunderstanding gap. To begin with, schools claim they do call unemployed teachers but they say that they don't respond.

The proof for this claim comes from interviews from school principals. SYNC-1: *"We call. We wait! They don't show up!"*

A-V transition to point 2: *Eerrruuup! :02-:03 (Money coming out of a cash machine).* VO: The union, however, claims the schools are more interested in saving money. They pay student-teachers 40% less than that they have to pay the others.

The proof for this claim comes from an interview with the union representative. SYNC-2: *"They're not telling the truth. The fact is they don't really care about unemployed teachers. They'd rather hire student teachers because they can pay them less and the students don't know their rights! But this is crazy because society is paying unemployment benefits!"*

A-V transition to point 3: *Fly-on-the-wall, the student teacher asks the class a question. "So what do you think when you read this?" (:02-:03).*

VO: The real reason student teachers are called might not have anything to do with money. The student teachers claim they have a better reputation.

The proof for this claim comes from a string of student teachers: SYNC-3 *"I've been given the impression that we're just better."* SYNC-4 *"I've been told that we're more up to date and perhaps a little smarter?"* SYNC-5 *"I've been called a lot. I'm happy to get the experience! Why do they call me? I don't know. They say I'm good!"*

Move the Story Forward!

Each issue is a "point" in its own chapter. Keep the points separate. Do not zig-zag! Do not go backwards by referring to a prior point. Move the story forward on a straight path. The last issue is clearly the most dramatic. It should be saved for last.

T3: The Conclusion that Summarises the Story

The VO returns to the general and gives a summary and consequences of the information in T2. This gives *perspective* and helps the viewer remember the information.

Reporter to camera: *"There're hundreds of unemployed teachers in the Hampton School District yet only a few of them work as substitutes. Instead they continue to collect unemployment insurance. The union blames the schools but the school district denies wrong-doing. No one we talked to could account for the statistics. Jonathan Cronin, the district's superintendent has agreed to meet next week with Michael Hobe, the union's president. (Carol Allen, at the Hampton School District office, Hampton County.")*

Question: wouldn't the story have a more dramatic ending to use SYNC-5 when the student teacher smiles and says: *"Why do they call me? I don't know. They say I'm good!"*

Obviously this is charming and perhaps more compelling than hearing from a neutral reporter. The problem is documentation is by definition a detail and by ending the story on a detail, the viewer loses sight of the big picture and the relevance of the story. In order for the story to be understood and remembered, it must end on the *general* not the specific. The reporter reminds the viewer that unemployed teachers are collecting unemployment insurance.

Still love that juicy sound bite from the student teacher? Save it as a tag for a documentary.

Best practice:
Don't end information-based stories on a SYNC

Story example 2: a terrible fire has destroyed both property and the plans for a celebrity charity boat race.

T-1: Angle: a fire in the eastern harbour of Marina del Rey is a double loss to the community.
T-2: Context: the harbour is relatively new, completed just two years ago; home to luxury boats of many movie stars; it was supposed to be the location of the 25th annual Soda Springs Charity Yacht Race.

T2: Development:
point 1: good fortune! No one was killed.
point 2: the fire destroyed fifty luxury boats, owned by the rich and famous.
point 3: arson is suspected. No one yet arrested.
T-3: Wrap and conclusion: no evidence of arson yet the charity event had enemies. Although no one was killed, there are thousands of victims.

Step-by-Step

A-V tease. Up from black to *fire at the harbour with fire engines; loud gushes of water mixed with gusts of flames. (:03-:04)*. VO: Saturday morning, 4 a.m., the eastern wing of Marina del Ray. Flames devour the berths including fifty luxury boats that leave a catastrophe in their wake. Estimated damage: 500 million Dollars. SYNC-1: (harbourmaster) *"It's one of the worst fires in the history of recreational boating. (Support). "Unbelievable! The work of the devil!"* (Colour).

T2: A-V transition to context: *large white sails flapping in the wind, FLAP FLAP FLUTTER! (:04)* Archive pictures and VO: The eastern wing of Marina del Ray's harbour is relatively new. It was completed just two years ago and was supposed to be the venue of the 25th annual Soda Springs Charity Yacht Race on June 15th. *(Fire engine siren! (:02)*. Now that's more than impossible. The charity event expected to raise 200 million dollars for muscular dystrophy. Sponsors must now find another venue in less than 30 days or cancel the event.

T2: A-V transition to Point 1: *fly-on-the-wall reportage of fire fighters with hoses: whoooooossssh! (:02-:03)*. VO: The fire started just after midnight and the yacht berths were the first to go. *(Fly-on-the-wall fire fighters: "Not here! You can't stand here! :03)*. VO: The fire burned fifty luxury boats beyond recognition. The good news is that no one was killed.

Documentation SYNC-2: (sailboat owner) *"We were supposed to sail for Hawaii today. We'd planned to spend the night on board but at the last minute we changed our minds. I just can't believe what's happened!"* (Support and colour).

T2: A-V transition to Point 2: *Workers clearing debris. Sweep! Sweep! :02)*. VO: This is berth 612, what used to be the home of Catalina Carrie, the 52 foot yawl, owned by actor, Tom Cruise. Mr. Cruise wasn't available for comment but his publicist says he's devastated. He isn't the only celebrity to lose a boat in Marina del Ray. David Beckham and Justin Timberlake are others.

Documentation SYNC-3: (harbourmaster): *"At least 20% of our clients are the rich and famous. It just goes to show that fires don't make distinctions or play favourites."* (Support and colour).

T2: A-V transition to Point 3: *Police radios :03-:04)*.
VO: As police investigate with massive assistance from the Coast Guard, there're rumours that arson was involved. There's some suspicion that a rival boating organisation might have been involved but there is absolutely no evidence of this at the moment.

(Police radios again :03). Two witnesses claim they saw shadowy figures in the area around midnight but no one can make a firm identification. Insurance companies need answers and so do the citizens of Marina del Ray.

Documentation SYNC-4: (police captain). *"Surveillance cameras will give us a lead. Otherwise, we're asking for everyone to come forward if they have any information at all."*

Best practice:
Respect transitions

Use A-V sound bites between points. Only :02-:04 allows the viewer to digest what's been offered so far. They also prepare them for what is coming next.

T3: Wrap and conclusion: reporter to camera: *"Authorities say this is one of the worst fires in the history of pleasure boating and if it turns out to be arson, one of the worse property crimes in California history. The victims are not just the boat owners, however, but the estimated 25,000 recipients who expected to benefit from the Charity Race in June. That's another 200 million dollars lost in the flames. (In Marina del Ray, Jackie Fuller for DR World Service.")* **A-V tag:** *sounds from cleanup crew.*

It might be tempting to end the story on SYNC-4, but then the issue of the charity race is forgotten. The story is better told if the reporter makes a summary and ties up the loose ends.

Consider an AV Tag

Add :02-:03 of NATURAL SOUND at the end the story if you have used a stand-up. This serves as a good transition to the studio anchor. Otherwise, it can be jarring to go from one size "talking head" to another.

Best practice:
End the story with an A-V tag

The 70–30 Rule

In short current affairs information-based stories, (2:30–6:00) the story is best told when the VO is approximately 70% and the interview segments are approximately 30%. If the interviews are lengthy (25–50 seconds) they dominate the story. When there is less VO, there are fewer pictures. Lengthy interviews are normal in radio journalism in which there are no pictures.

Question: why can't we use lengthy interviews and just cover them with pictures?

Answer: we can and this is frequently done. Journalists, however, are trained to condense and synthesize information. Interviews often ramble and take twice as long to say the same thing that a journalist's VO can say in half the time.

Best practice:
Information-based stories
70% VO
30% documentation syncs

7 Eye Level People Stories

Journalism needed a new model, which came to us through our print colleagues. It started with the Americans James Agee and John Hersey. Then came Tom Wolfe, Gay Talese and a long list of contemporary journalists who win Pulitzer Prizes. These are journalists who want to tell America the truth about itself beyond the framework of conventional objectivity.

In the printed form, this *narrative journalism* is sometimes called *literary journalism* because it demands a standard and quality of writing found only in literature. Offshoots are ethnographic or feature-travel journalism, reportage that doesn't pretend to be objective but does try to be fair.

Narrative journalism is growing in popularity and in some circles reaching messianic dimensions. Prize winning journalists passionately defend their craft and some claim it is only beginning to reach its potential.

A Liberal Social Agenda

Narrative journalists have a social conscience and they claim their mission is to remind us what it means to be human. Behind their efforts is a liberal social agenda to confront injustice by shining light into the dark corners of society. But facts alone, they say, do not inform. In the post-modern age, journalists must assign meaning.

How is this done? Eye level experience, they say. Participation in events and subsequent interpretation are required to break down the psychological barriers of apathy and cynicism. *Numinosity* – Carl Jung's term for emotional attention and heightened psychological awareness – is necessary for understanding.

A terminally ill man chooses assisted suicide to end his life. How does it feel? What does it mean for the rest of us? "Report for meaning," is what narrative journalists say. Reporters shouldn't fear evoking emotion. Detail makes stories come alive. Without them, it's just another love story or lost dog story.

At this point, we need to develop new language about story types. The primary contribution of narrative journalism was to depart from *reporting* and begin *storytelling*. In television, this might more accurately be called *people stories*. Instead of "top down" or outside looking in, these stories are told from "eye level," or from inside looking out.

These journalistic stories are an entirely different genre than traditional "human interest" stories. The topics of *people stories* are often serious, momentous and powerful. *Examples:* a farmer closes the door on his farm for the last time. A gay couple is officially married. A baby dies from having an HIV-positive mother. A daughter scores the winning point in a soccer game.

Fascination. DOI: 10.1016/B978-0-12-416037-8.00007-9

The assumption is that when the heart is engaged, the mind will follow. Once the viewers have seen the story, they will then be motivated to seek hard-core information that includes facts, experts, critics and analysis. Some TV stations might choose to run an information-based story on Monday and follow-up on Tuesday with a *people story* on the same topic. A better alternative might be to run the *people story* first and then, when the viewers' attention is engaged, follow with the information-based story.

> **Best practice:**
> Respect the supplementary relationship

Either way, it would be a grave mistake to think that eye level storytelling is replacing traditional reporting. Quite the contrary! The models supplement each other and broaden options, not narrow them. Eye level stories alone would preclude several genres of topics. Without reporting, a democratic public would remain uninformed about important events and developments. Storytelling was never meant to bump reporting to the sidelines and practitioners who claim otherwise are suffering from a serious misunderstanding.

Facts Are Not the Only Way to Inform

In eye level stories, the audience gets close to the topic not through facts, not through experts, and not through analysis but through the *personal experience* of the people who are central to the story. The journalist stops reporting and instead helps to produce the story subject's reality. It shows people to people and engages the heart, not just the mind.

Certainly, this is a departure from classical journalism but a welcome development. We live in the Information Age of a globalised world in which the average person is bombarded daily with masses of information. It's frequently overwhelming. Some people choose to go on "news fasts" and stop paying attention. Others become cynical and stop caring. Indeed, the assumed value of *people stories* is that they penetrate our resistance and evoke compassion in us.

> **Best practice:**
> Information alone does not inform

The Narrative Model in TV Journalism

People stories are not a new invention. In fact, they are a return to traditional documentary making. If one examines film history, it is clear that the traditional documentary was never detached or objective with two-sided reporting. Indeed, some purists claim a documentary is not a real documentary unless it challenges the smug assumptions of the existing establishment and disrupts the status quo.

We can take for example, Barbara Kopple's *Harlan County, USA* (1976), an icon of documentary making that never pretended to be objective. Had CNN or the BBC made the same story, it would have required interviews from "the other side" – Duke Power Company. Putting the employer on camera, however, would hardly advance the story. The exploitation of coalminers doesn't really have a credible defence. Thus, the "other side" would be predictable and add little information except, perhaps, to document greed.

Let's consider three people stories to see how they differ from traditional reporting.

Example 1: "Stoffers"

Stoffers is a small but well stocked general store in a suburb of Leeds, England. Brother and sister, Barker and Liz are the fourth generation to run this family business that for one hundred years has sustained the locals with food and hardware supplies. Most customers are friends and many of them survive on a line of credit. The little store is also a magnet for social life because twice a year, Barker and Liz host events to celebrate mid-summer and mid-winter. When a multinational corporation is given permission to build a mega-supermarket in their neighbourhood, the community faces disaster. How can they stop the corporation's plans? It's a classic David and Goliath story.

Fly-on-the-wall photography introduces us to Barker and Liz and to various members of the community. We spend time with these people and experience their sense of community. Stoffers is family to some of the residents who live in single room dwellings. We get to know Eddie and Marge and Lionel. We meet the children and grandchildren of Barker and Liz. We experience their frustration, anger and feelings of powerlessness in the face of corporate capitalism. "Trying to get this stopped is like holding back the ocean with a broom!" Barker says.

We are present at the last mid-summer festival and we sing hymns that are two hundred years old. We hear promises to hold the annual Christmas party but we also hear comments on property values and how many of the locals are being forced to sell their homes and move away. Six months later, we are there when the last customer pays his bills.

The story is 17:20 but not one minute of that time is devoted to lawyers, real estate experts or representatives from the corporation. Are we informed? Have we learned anything? It is arguable that what we witnessed is merely a slice of nostalgia. It is equally arguable that the power of global capitalism has never been so clearly expressed.

This eye level feature can serve as a debate starter for a studio wrap-around discussion and/or Part I in a series about gentrification of traditional neighbourhoods.

Example 2: "Hiding from her parents"

Amina is 19 and a second-generation Muslim immigrant in Denmark. She does well at gymnasium and wants to study medicine at university, but her parents have other plans for her. When she learns that she is promised in marriage to a second cousin, she runs away from home and this is where the story begins.

Amina lives in hiding and in fear for her life. An underground network of sympathisers protects her and others by giving them shelter, food and security. They accompany her to the university every day and wait for her to finish class.

After much persuasion, she allows us to visit and hear her story but only if her visual identity is protected. She tells us how much she misses her family, especially her little sister. Her mother has no idea where she is but keeps in touch by telephone. Amina suffers but she is not defeated. She understands the cultural conflict and explains it without bitterness.

Shahnaz is Amina's best friend, also Muslim but from a modern, progressive family. Shahnaz takes us into the student world and introduces us to other Muslim girls who are attending university. We go home with them and meet their parents. Fly-on-the-wall photography allows us to witness their conversations. Like their mothers, two of the girls observe *hijab* (wearing headscarves) and they demonstrate how to put the scarf on and tell us why they feel protected by wearing it. They take us to a local mosque to pray. They talk about their faith and why Mohammed would be proud that they're going to be professional women.

We meet Amina again who has just discovered that her brothers know where she is. She talks to Shahnaz about leaving Denmark. We see her for a last time at the airport.

The story is 16:35. We never hear from experts, politicians or religious authorities but we are much wiser for having spent time with Amina and Shahnaz.

Example 3: "The elderly engineer who wanted to die"

German engineer, Ernest-Karl Aschmoneit is 81 years old, in the early advanced stages of Parkinson's disease and wants to end his life. He is a member of Dignitas, a Swiss organisation that provides professional "assisted suicide" through a lethal dose of sodium pentobarbital, offered in a glass to be drunk voluntarily.

In 2003, Aschmoneit flies to Zurich. He agrees to allow TV journalists to accompany him on his last journey because – as he says on camera – he wants other countries to establish assisted suicide programmes and he feels his own story can be used effectively for promotion of this controversial practice.

The American network, CBS arrived in Zurich with a large consortium of producers, journalists and technicians. Two other TV journalists on the story were Christian Degn and Anders Rostgaard, two young Danish journalists who were working freelance.

CBS produced a traditional journalistic top down story, a critical examination of the issues that was broadcast on its flagship current affairs programme, *60 Minutes*. Degn's and Rostgaard's treatment of the story was a *people story* and broadcast on TV2's *Dags Dato*. A close examination of the story's two different treatments reveals the differences between reporting and storytelling.

"Suicide Tourists" (CBS, 2003)

Predictably, the *60 Minutes* version is high, very high, on the scale for *information*. The story covers all the obvious ethical issues – of which there are many – begging, even screaming to be addressed. Ernest-Karl Aschmoneit is introduced early as the case study but since he is merely an illustration of the issue, he gets only 30% of screen time.

Instead, attention quickly shifts to the founder and director of Dignitas, Ludwig A. Minelli who evaluates all candidates for assisted suicide. The journalist questions his competence and gets him to admit that he makes judgment on instinct. Minelli claims to have no doubts about what he is doing: "Ah, it is not knowing," he says. "It is feeling, and that is much better than knowing." As to doubts, he says, "I have no bad dreams. I do not wake up with bad ideas about what I'm doing." Does that give him a sense of power? "It has nothing to do with power. It's just humanity. Helping people with pain."

Then we hear from psychiatrist Thomas Schlaepfer, a specialist in depression who is not opposed to assisted suicide but is critical of the way Dignitas operates. "If somebody flies into Zurich Airport, is brought into an interview for an hour and prescribed medication, that's totally wrong," he says. "That's ethically wrong. Legally, it might be OK in Swiss law, but ethically it's wrong." Schlaepfer says it is "totally impossible" to find out in a brief visit or two whether someone is of sound mind.

The most serious question facing Dignitas, however, concerns mentally ill people like Walter Wittwer, a schizophrenic. For 10 years, Wittwer was a member of another assisted suicide group that wouldn't allow him to take his life because he was mentally ill. Then Wittwer joined Dignitas and three months later, he was dead. Minelli argues that mentally ill people have the same right to take their own lives as others: "You can't say and you shouldn't say that mentally ill people should not have human rights."

Next is Helmut Eichenburger, a retired urologist who prescribes the overdose for Dignitas' members. He says emotions matter. "A lot of people feel lonely and they say: *Well, I have nothing more. I have no relatives; I have no friends, no life. Why am I still living?* That's when I say that the dying has begun."

The debate continues when psychiatrist Schlaepfer says that suicidal tendencies are often a symptom of mental illness and can be treated. "In this office," he says, "many people have said: *I'm totally depressed. I want to end my life* and weeks later this opinion was changed."

Finally, we hear from public prosecutor, Andreas Brunner, who believes the law is dangerously unregulated, giving him little room to act. "These days, everyone – even you or me, we – can make assisted suicides," says Brunner, noting that nothing – not even a medical degree – is required to start an organisation that helps people kill themselves.

After this discussion of the ethical issues, Ernest-Karl is given the overdose of barbiturate, which he drinks behind a closed door and within an hour he is dead. We see his body in a body bag as it is removed from the clinic.

CBS's version is loaded with *information*. TV journalism students who see the *60 Minutes* version rely on the high information content to keep themselves emotionally detached. The result is a substantive discussion of medical ethics, courage, illness and cognitive decision-making.

"The Last Journey" (Den Sidste Rejse, 2003, TV2)

The Danish version of the same story prioritised *identification* over information. Indeed, the information component is minimal. Only the basic facts are given
to establish context. Ernest-Karl Aschmoneit is not just an *illustration* of the issue
but the *focus* of the story. The only other interview in the story is from Ludwig A.
Minelli who vigorously defends his organisation with animated indignation.

In the Danish version, there are no on-screen critics of Minelli's role or of
Dignitas' procedures. There is no discussion about depression and its relationship to
being of *sound mind*. Thus the Danish version is *information* poor, in spite of the fact
it is two minutes longer than the CBS story.

We meet Ernest-Karl up close and learn a lot about him. He is not a religious man
and has no belief in an afterlife. He had a good career as a mechanical engineer and
a happy marriage but he is not sentimental and no longer gets inspiration from looking at old photographs. He describes his present life, how he can't sleep and how he
dreads the progression of his disease.

His intelligence is obvious and there is no problem understanding why he worries
about the indignity of losing his mental faculties. He is a sweet man, unexpectedly charming and thoroughly engaging. He "quacks" with the ducks at the pond. He describes
how he has cleaned his apartment, taken out the rubbish and placed the key through the
mail slot. He talks about the need to carry a suitcase in order to avoid suspicion from the
authorities that he worries might try to stop him. In astonishingly good humour, he meets
friends at Hamburg Airport to say goodbye and jokes with the ticket clerk who wishes
him a good journey, totally unaware why this man is travelling to Zurich.

In this eye level *people story*, the viewer gets to *experience* Ernest-Karl's decision. When he drinks the pentobarbital, we have personal reactions to his decision. In
fact, *identification* is so high, the viewer simply suspends critical judgment about the
issues the story raises.

After screening the Danish version, many students sit in stunned silence.
Reactions are mixed. Emotions are high. Some students are deeply touched and
impressed with the storytelling. Others insist that this version is not really journalism. "It's not balanced!" they claim. "It's an advocacy story!"

In relation to *identification*, however, some might say that the Danish version is
superior storytelling. Did 81 year-old Ernest-Karl Aschmoneit have the right to com-
mit suicide? Does society have the right to prevent it? Is it humane to make people live longer than they want to? Who decides? And which version of journalism
gets us closer to the issues? A more provocative question might be: had we not met
Ernest-Karl and experienced his situation, would we even pay attention to the core
issue? A people story wakes us up and commands our attention.

Personality-Driven Journalism

The *people stories* that one can see on American television are generally not documentaries but short inspirational stories (2:15) that teach us something about our

common humanity. Some of them are light and humorous. Some are serious. A high percentage of them however, require the participation of a personality, either on camera or in a highly animated VO.

America has a long list of TV journalists who are famous for their work but this particular style isn't always applicable in many European cultures where projection of personality is considered inappropriate to journalism.[1]

Some American consultants who teach workshops in Europe say they always find compelling, engaging people who are willing to go about their business while being photographed for *people stories*. That's one half of the equation. What about TV journalists who are eager to perform on camera and project their personalities? Can they use their voices to tell a story in a compelling manner?[2]

There are a few European TV journalists who are eager to imitate what they see in personality-driven American style stories but their enthusiasm is controversial and the substance for emotionally charged discussions. Should they be encouraged to try? Or is it altogether inappropriate?

Maybe it's time to reconsider the role of the TV journalist. Why *should* it be inappropriate to use personality to enhance fascination? (See Chapter 10.)

Personalities Not Necessarily Required

Some people stories, however, do not require personalities. Indeed, many eye level stories keep the journalist's on-camera presence to a minimum. Some stories restrict the journalist's participation to minimal VO narration while others see the journalist's role merely as an "arranger" behind the scenes. It would be unfortunate indeed to dismiss eye level features on the premise that they are categorically "too American."

The Value of Emotion

In spite of deeply rooted allegiance to traditional, top down TV reporting, the *people story* is here to stay. Its value for communication is obvious. When journalists dare to be emotional, communication is rapid, satisfying and complete. *People stories* break down emotional barriers and allow us to feel our mutual humanity. Its application to serious stories is possible and when used effectively, excellent television.

The emotional value of eye level stories does not come without a price, however. See chapter 12 for a discussion of the ethical considerations concerning this story style.

---

[1] See Chapter 10 on the role of the TV journalist.
[2] In my generation, it was Charles Kuralt and Edward R. Morrow. Today it might be Steve Hartman, Richard Quest or Jeanne Moos.

Do People Stories Have a Limit?

The central debate about eye level storytelling is in the application to BBI topics. Some journalists claim that *storytelling* can be applied to any story, regardless of the topic. Others say that this technique can be applied only to topics that are "sexy" with instant appeal to the viewer. The debate continues.

8 Words Vs. Pictures

Writing the Current Affairs Story

Writing for TV journalism is not restricted to language. Writing refers primarily to *structure* and the writer's different tools. Words are only one tool. Pictures, NATURAL SOUND, editing tempo and the use of interviews are the other tools. Thus, we can say that TV journalists fall into two categories: word writers and audio-video writers. The best TV journalists are both.

Silence can also be a tool. Good writers know that many of our vocabularies are wordless and silent. A person in an interview might sound calm and relaxed but a cutaway to his hands will show fidgeting fingers and white knuckles. The same is true for a frown or grimace. All of these are wordless vocabularies.

A-V sound bites are another tool. They take the viewer into the story and engage them emotionally to the event. Even as little as 2 seconds make a difference.

An appropriate bit of advice for TV journalists is to find ways to avoid using words. You might want to tell the journalist: "stop talking so much!"

- Do it inside the points
- Do it as transitions between points
- Do it between and inside chapters

Best practice:
Let the pictures and sound breathe!

Writing *to* Pictures

Ask yourself: what do the pictures make me say? Imagine this: it's Christmas Eve at the airport and all flights are cancelled due to dense fog. You wander around the airport and observe. What's happening? What do you see? People are angry, bored and frustrated, yes, but it's the children you notice more than the adults. You shoot video fly-on-the-wall while talking to children between 1 and 10 years old.

Example: a ten-year-old girl has just finished reading the same book for the fourth time. Her face says it all.

Journalist off cam: "Boring?"
Sync: "Yeah, boring!"
Journalist off cam: "How boring?"
Sync: "On a scale of 1–10, it's a 10."
A five year old is sliding out of her seat onto the floor.

Fascination. DOI: 10.1016/B978-0-12-416037-8.00008-0

VO: "Little Emily's *had* it!"

The baby has just taken his first step!

VO: "And so it went like this. All flights cancelled. Little Jacob: right on schedule!"[1]

Example: in 2004, Chechen terrorists held 300 hostages, mainly children, in a Beslan school while their parents waited outside.

VO: At last, a sign that the hostage takers were listening. The youngest, always the most vulnerable, carried out one by one to safety....a brief glimmer of hope... offering so little...It's the quiet that hits you first... and the occasional sob that breaks the silence... They watch and wait...but there's nothing to see. Their worst fears come when they ear sounds like this (bomb explodes)....like a bullet through the heart, some say.[2]

Some of the best writing is when the words are used to support the pictures and *awaken the senses*: Compare the two following sentences:[3]

"It was a clear day, and the wind wasn't blowing."

"The day dawned as still and clear, as if the sky intended to hold its breath."

The poetic aspect of the second sentence supports brilliant photography of dawn. The photography has to be good, however, to justify the poetic language. Otherwise, it sounds overdone, compensatory, and absurd.

Writing *for* Pictures

Information-based stories often require you to write the script first and then find representational pictures to illustrate it.

As you read in Chapter 6, information-based stories have a *context* section in which you give background to the issue, providing an explanation for why you're telling the story. This *context* segment is usually the part where you need strong writing and suitable illustrations. Some stories, however, need a list of pictures from start to finish.

Example: the fire service has started an information campaign about toxic chemicals in the home and they ask you to produce a documentary called *"Information is the Best Defence."* This is the kind of story for which you need specific visuals and most of them must be constructed, as opposed to fly-on-the wall. After researching the story, you write the script and then think about what pictures you need to make it "television." Many of the pictures will be illustrations of the words you are saying.

Re-read Chapter 4 about story treatment. The story about toxic chemicals is classic BBI. This is when your *fascination* tools are critically important. Brief A-V bites are needed to create engagement.

---

[1] John Larson, KOMO News 4; screened at the NPPA Video News Workshop, March 22, 1995.
[2] Sky News reporter, Rachel Amatt, 2004.
[3] Most examples quoted in this chapter are from Frederick Shook, *Television Newswriting*.

Combo Style

In fact, most TV journalism stories use a combination of both types: writing: *to* pictures and *for* pictures.

Example: the story is about Slovak gypsies who need adequate housing. The journalist and photographer have returned to the TV station with two cassettes of fly-on-the-wall photography. An apartment building designed for four families is home to thirty-five people. The pictures have strong images and animated interviews.

The journalist previews all the footage and asks: what do they *make* me say? After writing the script, the journalist decides that certain other pictures are needed to write the context part of the story plus small portions in the development section. If archive footage is available, the pictures can be borrowed. Otherwise, the reporter tells the photographer: "go get me" (please!) XY and Z in order to complete the story. This asks for constructed pictures that are used to illustrate information in the VO.

Writing for the Ear. It's a Conversation

No matter what language – English, German, Spanish or Dutch, etc. – writing must be crisp and clear in simple short sentences without dependent clauses. The best TV writing is when the reporter talks *to* the viewers, not *at* them. In this way, it is a *conversation*. Compare the two following sentences:

1. "The city council agreed Friday to apply for national funds to assist small businesses in the Arab community by giving them low interest loans."
2a. "Arab businesses are struggling and the city council thinks it's found a way to help." *(Oh, yeah?)* (**room walla** of council meeting).
2b. "Politicians want to apply for special funds at the national level." *(That's a good idea!)* " This would give low interest loans to immigrant businesses and kick-start their economy." *(Great! That should definitely help!))*

Some Rules for Writing for the Ear

1. Write short sentences with one thought per sentence. Be careful, however, not to make all sentences the same length because, when spoken, they can produce a staccato effect that is unpleasant to the ear.
2. Use ACTIVE verbs that stress the doer of the action; passive verbs stress the recipient of the action. Most languages have both. Avoid the passive verbs in TV writing because it softens the impact of the broadcast copy.

Compare the two following sentences:

Fifty demonstrators **were arrested** while burning the American flag and trying to overturn a police car.

Police **arrested** fifty demonstrators while they burned the American flag and tried to overturn a police car.

3. Avoid dependent clauses.
4. Avoid parenthetical phrases.
5. Avoid referring to prior information. All information should move forward.
6. Write in "layers." Give one fact at a time.
7. Beware of "time" references.

Don't let a time reference dangle at the end of a sentence, if it is important to the story. Keep it close to the main verb. Consider the two following sentences.

University students may think twice about skipping classes **this autumn**.
University students may think twice **this autumn** about skipping classes.

In the preceding example, the story is about a new policy concerning low attendance that begins **this autumn**. If the story was about low attendance in general, it wouldn't matter where the time reference showed up in the sentence.

8. Avoid writing more than the pictures or interviews can support.
9. Beware of words that could collide with pictures.

(See the section about action vectors in Chapter 3.)

10. Avoid jargon in your descriptions. Use only words that the average person understands.
11. For those who write in English, do not begin sentences with the word *however*.

Lyrical Writing Awakens the Senses

Some words create imagery. They paint pictures in our mind because they help us *sense* the things that are described. Bob Dotson is an American NBC news correspondent. Here are some samples of his writing.[4]

"Katie Osage was as thin as a dying moon."

"He was a slight man with a face that could sell Marlboros."

"To find Art Brothers, you go west to Salt Lake City, turn left and drive for the rest of your life."

"Their time is cut in tiny slices. Too thin for thought."

Use Ordinary Language

Compare the following sentences.

"Airline officials say 'lack of visibility' caused the crash."

<u>or</u>

"Airline officials blame the crash on thick fog."

General Motors reports that automotive production declined last month.

<u>or</u>

General Motors says it made fewer cars last month.

[4] Quoted in *Television Newswriting*, Frederick Shook, page 27.

Tight Writing

International students who study TV journalism at DSMJ are encouraged to produce stories in their native languages. They work in teams of two and notice immediately that there are differences in the length of time to say the same thing. German, for example, usually takes more words than English. Regardless of the language used in a VO, however, all writing should be as efficient as possible.

Here is an example in English.

VO: "He said that the cutbacks in the healthcare field had placed hospitals in a crisis situation."

Cut out the following words:

That. Back. The. Field. A. Situation.

"He said the cuts in healthcare had placed hospitals in crisis."

Six words have been removed. Seventeen words are cut down to twelve. One third or 33%.[5]

Transitions Between Studio and Story

After an A-V tease (:02-:03) the first sentence tells us what the story is. If your focus is clear, this is usually the same idea as that which the viewer heard from the studio presenter. *Avoid using the same words.*

Example: studio presenter: "The Spanish went to the polls Sunday to vote in a new government. There were few surprises as the socialists won a clear majority. Now some voters are claiming it was a rigged election. Isabella Lopez has the story.

Up from black to **A-V tease: *street walla of a political demonstration*.**

VO: Democracy in Spain could be in trouble. Thousands of demonstrators took to the streets over the weekend to protest last Sunday's election. A petition campaign has already collected fourteen thousand signatures and it's just the beginning.

Leading to a Sync as Documentation

SYNCS are documentation. They support the claim made by the journalist in the VO. *Avoid using the same words as in the sync.*

Example: VO: Danes work 37 hours a week, three hours less than in Lithuania. *To increase the hourly working standard in Denmark, however, would be difficult. **Such decisions can't be made by politicians**.*

SYNC: (Danish professor of employment law:) ***"This decision can't be made by the politicians**. It's the labour unions and employers who decide."*

This is jarring for the viewer's ear. You have no control over the exacts words in the sync but you can use different words to lead into it.

---

[5] Neil Everton. *JV Handbook*, page 74.

Example: VO: *Danes work 37 hours a week, three hours less than in Lithuania. To increase the hourly working standard in Denmark, however, would be difficult.*

Now the SYNC tells why.

SYNC: (Danish professor of employment law:) ***"This decision can't be made by the politicians.*** *It's the labour unions and employers who decide*

Some Rules for Recording the VO

- Sit or stand in an active mode.
- Use your hands to gesture while recording.
- Choose a tempo and tone that is appropriate to the story.
- Use your voice as a ":" (colon) to support the SYNC.
- Don't be intimidated by the microphone!

9 Using Interviews

There are basically three types of interviews for stories, each for a different purpose. (1) Research and background (2) verification of facts from a second or third source, and (3) videotaped interviews from which you will extract segments (SYNCS) to document the claims that are made by the journalist.

How Do You Get People to Talk to You?

One of the more challenging tasks in TV journalism is persuading people to talk to you, first as research and then, (and here's the difficult part), on camera.

Do not assume cooperation. Many stories have been lost at this critical point because the journalist was too eager to get started.

Research interviews require the cooperation of someone who might not end up in the story. Some people prefer not appearing on camera. Others feel offended if they are not included in the recorded version. "The media" has become so powerful, however, that some people enjoy frustrating TV journalists by refusing to cooperate. Friendly persuasion is required.

- **Be assertive but never aggressive!** If you are looking for an expert from an organisation, go directly to the top and then work down. When using the telephone, if the person you want is speaking on another line, don't hang up. Tell the secretary that you'll wait.

  When looking for case studies, you often go to appropriate organisations for contacts. If an agency cannot give out names, give your name and number and ask for someone to call you back, if they're interested. *But don't expect people to immediately return your call.* Likewise, don't just send an e-mail and then sit back and wait. People are busy. People are shy. Follow up your initial contact with another call or e-mail.
- **Be polite!** Treat the interview subject with respect. Begin by identifying yourself and saying what you're doing. Then ask: *"do you have time to talk to me right now?"* If it is a research interview over the telephone, say so by telling the person that you are still collecting information. If you know that the person is perfect to document a point, be prepared to solicit their cooperation. Find out when they are available. Make a firm appointment and say how much time you need. Be realistic. Get an address and explicit directions so you arrive on time.
- **Pay attention to the source.** A press officer or a public affairs manager may be one step away from the person you want to interview and may have reasons for putting you off. Likewise, a "mouthpiece" of an organisation is paid to give you an official line. This is particularly true of press conferences.
- **Give people the opportunity to give their side of story.** Sometimes the source may be someone who feels misunderstood. This is their chance to "set the record straight."

Fascination. DOI: 10.1016/B978-0-12-416037-8.00009-2

Research

This is the first step. Often beginner TV journalists are so eager to start shooting they forget the cardinal rule:

Do not assume anything!

The very first thing in the production plan is information gathering: on the internet; with experts; and other relevant sources. Crosscheck the assertions and verify facts. Then and only then do you identify your angle. The angle gives the story its focus and will be the "umbrella" over the claims that the reporter makes in the VO.

Question: what happens if my research doesn't support my angle?

Answer: you have two choices: drop the story and find another or find a new angle, one that is supported by your research.

Golden Rule: if your story is failing at the research level, drop it! It can only get worse.

Don't Videotape Research Interviews

Videotaping research interviews is not the best way to gather information. Firstly, interviews in a research phase might require long conversations and involve talking to many people. If you videotape these interviews, you eat up a lot of tape. In order to assure accuracy, use a small audio tape recorder or take comprehensive notes by hand.

Secondly, sources are usually more relaxed when they are not on camera, resulting in more thoughtful answers.

Don't Edit Research Interviews into the Story

Research interviews are not normally efficient. People repeat themselves or get tangential, wandering from the point and taking a long time to answer the question. A research interview may take as long as one hour. As print journalists well know, information from an interview must be digested and then synthesized. A VO from a skilled TV journalist can say in fifteen seconds what the interviewed person said in forty-five.

Managing the Interview in Information-Based Stories: *Syncs* and *Sound Bites*

Do videotape documentation interviews but never start with a question that you want answered. This makes the person feel "used" and is not the best way to get cooperation. *Smoooze*. Make small talk and develop rapport by treating the subject as a human being, not merely a "source." Then roll tape and start to record.

As we said in Chapter 2, statements from interviews are called "syncs" because the sound is synchronised with the movement of the person's lips. Syncs can be any length. A short, concise sync is called a "sound bite." In other words, all sound bites are syncs but not all syncs are sound bites.

In most European cultures, a sound bite is 10–20 seconds. (In the USA, they can be as short as :02) Some interview bites give facts. Others give "colour" to the claims by offering opinions or emotional reactions. Both are documentation.

In top down feature stories, reporters ask off-camera research questions to gather background information for VOs. On-camera questions find the emotion in the story. Don't waste time and tape asking who, what, when and where? Those are research questions. Instead, ask: "how does it feel when you're dancing to African rhythms?" And "can you tell me why you wanted to adopt a baby from Latin America?"

In information-based stories, the goal of the interview is to get documentation. There are several ways to get effective documentation so that the journalist does not give away control. Follow these simple rules:[1]

- *Be prepared.* Research! Research! Research! Plan your questions. Know what it is you want to document. Information-based stories work best when they are sharply angled; when they go deeper instead of wider. You will lose the sharpness of your angle if you include many interviews that take you into different directions.
- *Avoid phrasing questions that can be answered with "yes" or "no."* Such answers have little information and are difficult to edit. Make the subject speak in full sentences. Avoid questions that start with *do, did, can, could,* etc. Instead, ask questions that start with *what? why? how?*
- *Ask only one question at a time; never piggyback.* *Example*: "How long do you think it will take for the ballots to be counted and do you feel it is the right procedure?" The subject seldom answers both questions and usually answers only the easier one.
- *Avoid phrasing questions with provocative language.* "Why are you being so impatient when you have a whole month to get it done?" The subject might react to one word or phrase ("impatient") and lose focus, never getting around to answering the question.
- *Avoid questions that involve several sentences.* "Last week you said that the new union contract would never be accepted and now you say that it might be but only after a month of negotiation and even then, there could be problems with some members whom you refuse to identify and...."
- *Keep it simple:one idea at a time.* "When do you think the new contract will be approved? Why have you changed your mind? Who are the members you expect will say no?"
- *Avoid putting words into the subject's mouth.* "Are you disappointed?" Don't interpret feelings. Let the person say it. Ask: "How do you feel?"
- *Listen to the answers!* You can ask follow-up questions if you are paying attention. Make sure the question is answered. Otherwise, ask it again.
- *Think of a hand-in-glove*: A sound bite must fit the claim immediately preceding it in the VO narration. Otherwise, it does not advance the story.
- *Ask one final question:* "Is there anything else you'd like to say?" *Sometimes this is when you hit gold.*

[1] Neil Everton, *Making Television News,* pages 41–42.

Videotaping Your Documentation Interviews

Good editing starts with good shooting. Think of the possibilities as they relate to the human body:

> The whole body, head to toe: LS
> Head to below the knees: MLS
> Head to hips: MS
> Head and shoulders: MCU
> Head with shoulders but cut across forehead: CU
> Parts of the face, nose, eyes, etc.: XCU

The conventional framing of an interview is a head and shoulders shot (MCU) with the face turned three-quarters to the lens showing two eyes but not always two ears. Remember *the nipple rule:* all human beings have breast nipples in the same place. An easy way to frame a MCU is to cut across the breast line and allow for headroom.

Best practice:
Frame interviews in an MCU

No Profiles, Please!

It is counter-productive to shoot an interview on a profile. How can a person be engaging if he is looking into space? Think of the camera as an extension of the journalist. She should be able to poke out her elbow and feel the shoulder of the photographer. If she can't, the camera is too far away. The greater the distance between the journalist and the camera, the greater is the profile on the subject. Frame interviews so the viewer gets two eyes. This maximises engagement.

Pay Attention to Eye Contact

Keep eye contact on an even plane, assuring equality between the journalist and the interviewee. Most people measure the same from the waist up and the differences in height are mainly in the legs. It is recommended to shoot interviews from a sitting down position.

No Guillotine Shots, Please!

Media aesthetics dictate places where the human body may be cut without offending sensibilities. The human neck is one place to avoid. Viewers do not like to watch a "severed head" that is detached from its neck and shoulders. Pay attention to framing and do *not* cut people off at the vulnerable parts of their body: neck, waist, knees or ankles.

When You Want Intensity

If an ultra extreme close-up (XXCU) is desired on the interview, frame by cutting in the middle of the forehead and across the chin. Preferable is the less intense XCU that frames across the forehead and includes a little bit of shoulders.

Be Careful About Extreme Close-Ups in Interviews. Think About Chocolate!

It's true that intensity creates engagement but the same engagement can evaporate, if used to excess. Think of eating nothing but chocolate all day long. The first time, it's delicious. The second time, it tastes good but not as good as the first time. By third or fourth time, it's starting to lose its ability to give pleasure. How long does intensity sustain engagement? If over-used, intensity burns itself out. Worse, it causes irritation.

Extreme CUs on interviews work the same way. If you over-use them, they start to lose their power to engage or to intensify. In addition, if you begin the interview with an XCU and you want to intensify it, you have nowhere to go.

Lighting the Interview

The human face is one of the most interesting subjects we can photograph in TV journalism. Eyes are the most important feature: poets call them "windows into the soul." It's not always possible to control the lighting but when it is, light the face so that it engages the viewer as much as possible.

- Flat lighting is not as interesting as lighting that gives contrast and sculptures the face. Use artificial light or if outdoors, place the subject under a tree that filters sunlight.
- Separate the person's head from the background. Artificially, a lamp casts light on the edge of the hair. Without a lamp, place the subject against a background lighter than the hair colour.
- "Catch-light" in the eyes makes the interview engaging. Look for the small pin-point of light, a reflection from the eyes' water. Shoot at an angle where it is visible.
- Avoid "raccoon" faces. These small, bear-like creatures have sweet faces, but human faces cannot communicate when the eyes are black slits or look like they're blindfolded. Interviews shot in bright sunlight run the risk of losing the eyes. If necessary, move the person into the shadows.

Editing the Interview

The answer to a question might take up to two full minutes but you want to use the first 8 seconds, the middle 15 seconds and then the final 9 seconds. The sound might flow freely across the two edits, but the face in the picture would leap about the screen in a jump cut. What do you do? *Use a cutaway!* There are several options to cover the edits in an interview.

A Reverse Shot of the Journalist

Called a "noddy" in the UK, this is standard practice in Anglo-American broadcast industries and is never questioned. Modern application of this reverse discourages the nodding head, however, because it can be misinterpreted as subjective agreement. The alternative is to see the journalist merely *listening*.

If you wish to use this reverse, make sure that you do not cross the axis line. Otherwise, both people will be looking in the same direction.

If the subject (A) is looking LEFT to RIGHT, the listening journalist (B) must be looking RIGHT to LEFT.

If the camera crosses the line, the speakers will be shown facing the same way. Both of them are listening to a third person and not to one another.

LS of the Journalist and the Interview Subject

Shoot far enough way so that you can't see their lips moving. This is effective because the interview does not leave the location. The edit maintains the integrity and intimacy of the one-on-one conversation.

CU of Hands Gesticulating or Clutching Something

This cutaway is often ridiculed but it is practical and effective if it fits the story. *Example*: a priest talks about his vows of celibacy. He feels nervous and fidgets with the rope on his belt. If we have seen his belt in the wider shot, the cutaway works perfectly.

Pictures that Illustrates the Subject's Comments

This is a common cutaway but it moves the interview into another location. As an example, the viewer leaves the cosy setting of the conversation and is transported into a tribal war in Somalia, a meeting of world leaders in Korea or a hurricane. This technique works best if the cutaway is sustained and the interview becomes a VO.

An Object in the Room Where the Interview Is Taking Place

A book. A report. An empty hospital bed. Dishes of food. These cutaways work best if the object has been seen in a prior shot.

Question: how do I edit an interview, if I don't want to be seen and I don't want to use cutaways?

Answer: divide the question into sections, shooting each part in different sized shots. For example, inter-cut from LS to a MCU size shot to a CU, etc. An alternative is to use a dissolve to cover the jump-cut.

Continuity

Pay attention to what the subject is wearing. You might find it necessary to edit from different interviews taken at different times. In the first one, the man is wearing a red shirt but in the second, he is wearing a raincoat and his reading glasses. Edit those two parts together and the result will be distracting, to say the least.

Keeping Control of the Story

Even experienced TV journalists shoot interviews that are not used in the final edit. It takes practice to learn which interviews are needed and which ones are not. Journalists fall in love with some of their subjects and it takes courage to know when you have to "kill a darling." Ask yourself one simple question: *does this interview advance the story?* If not, don't use it.

When Syncs Don't Fit the VO

Remember the hand in a glove; or using another analogy, the sync sound bite is like a boxcar attached to a locomotive on the same track. Consider what happens when the sound bite moves to another track.

Example: returning to our story about substitute teachers and the labour union.

VO: Schools pay student teachers 40% less than regular teachers. The union claims this is why they hire them as substitutes. They just want to save money, they say.

EMPTY SYNC: "That's a mean thing to say! I'm really offended. And they're my union too!"

This colour statement doesn't address the claim in the VO immediately preceding it. Either the schools want to save money or they don't! The hand is not sliding into the glove. The statement is moving to a different track. Therefore, *it cannot advance the story.* Using sound bites in this way is sloppy journalism.

Remember 70–30 for Information-Based Stories

As we said earlier, in information-based stories, it is wise to limit the interview syncs to no more than 30% of the story, each bite no more than 15–20 seconds. There are two good reasons for this.

1. When an information-based story uses more than 30% syncs it means that *other people* are telling the story, not the journalist. If the SYNCS are as much as 70%, this reduces the journalist to a mere postman who is delivering a letter without actively participating in the story. Short information-based stories require the *participation* of a trained and skilled journalist.
2. Information learned in the interview can be written into the VO narration and then used with *pictures*, making it more television and less "radio with pictures."

Have Confidence in Your Research!

Using long interviews is a frequent mistake of beginners and this is usually the result of undeveloped confidence. ("Who am I to say? I need an expert.")

Confident and experienced TV journalists interview widely and deeply in order to learn the subject. If claims are controversial, they get verification from a second or third source before using the material. Then they write the information into a VO and carefully select interviews to *document* the claims.

Example: let's return one more time to the story about substitute teachers and the labour union. After conducting considerable research, the reporter says:

VO: We talked to ten schools and they agreed that student teachers are called in as substitutes. They also admitted that they pay student teachers 40% less than regular teachers. This was appropriate, they said, because student teachers are not yet fully qualified. So why call them in the first place? We were told that they're reliable and smart.

SUPPORT SYNC:

School principal: *"Yes. We call them! And they come! They're reliable and they're also up to date on all the subjects they teach!"* (:06)

SUPPORT SYNC:

Student teacher: *"I don't mind the lower pay because it's good experience."* (:03)

COLOR SYNC:

Union representative: *"It's not right! The student teachers should be studying! Not taking the jobs of professionals!"* (:04)

When Syncs Are Factually Untrue

Avoid using interview sound bites that say things that are factually untrue. This is sloppy journalism and might confuse the viewer.

Example: in the story about the Danish 190% tax on cars, a Danish citizen/consumer might express his displeasure about the tax by saying something like this: SYNC: *"It's really terrible! You end up paying almost triple what you'd pay in the USA for the same car. And you don't get anything in return!"*

The exceptionally high tax on cars is used to finance the Danish welfare state and it is factually untrue that Danes do not benefit from it. *An untrue statement cannot move the story forward.*

In addition, since the story is produced for a foreign audience, it's irresponsible to use this last sentence in the interview. Viewers in Spain, Holland, the United Kingdom, etc. would receive incorrect information.

Interviewing Children

There is an old saying among veteran TV journalists: *beware children and animals!* These two groups are difficult to work with because they don't follow directions and give us what we want. Unless the child is an exception, he or she will respond to a TV interview with downcast eyes and short, almost monosyllabic answers.

Is there anything one can do to make it easier?

One veteran TV educator suggests this: show the child the TV equipment and microphones before you start to record. Record a few seconds of something and then play it back so the child can see it on the screen. Put the headphones on and let the child hear what NATURAL SOUND is like. Then you can begin the interview. The best ones with children normally occur when the questions are quite specific.

Example: a little girl with leukaemia has gone to Disney World for the first and probably the last time. She meets Mickey Mouse and Donald Duck. Minnie Mouse gives her a hug and the little girl kisses Minnie's big nose. The interview works better if the journalist asks: "What did Minnie's nose feel like?" than if the child is asked: "What did you like best about Disney World?"[2]

Example: a kindergarten just got a pet pig.

Up from black to **A-V tease**: *oink oink! and children giggling.* VO: Porky here is a new student at Smith's Elementary School. She arrived yesterday and already has made new friends.

Why isn't this an eye level story? The answer is children are not normally articulate. There are exceptions but it could be excessively time-consuming to find a child to tell the story when you're up against a deadline. Top down stories are more efficient. You can get good colour syncs but don't expect a child to tell the story.

Interviewing Teenagers

Adolescents offer the TV journalist a different problem. They might not be shy but they are acutely self-conscious and because they are, they have a tendency to posture; to play a role. Most of all, they have to appear "cool." This means they don't always say what they really mean. Interviewing teenagers requires exceptional preparation and a firm agreement on what is going to be said. You might sacrifice some spontaneity, but you get a higher degree of authenticity.

How to Get Good Sound Bites from Shy Subjects

A face-to-face *interview* is not always the best way to get good sound bites. People freeze and become self-conscious. The spontaneity that you heard on the telephone suddenly disappears.

1. Use fly-on-the-wall to shoot a group discussion that is guided by a skilled leader. Ask the questions that will produce the answers you need to be used as VO. Make sure you are working with an agile and competent sound technician with a boom microphone who can aim it appropriately.

Remember the story about Camp Fjordmark for overweight children? (Chapter 5). The story was produced at eye level in spite of the fact that getting informative interviews from children is difficult. The VO material when Anna and Sarah talk about

---

[2] From Frederick Shook, *Television Newswriting*, pages 110–111.

one another, for example, was recorded not in interviews but in a fly-on-the-wall session during which the girls were asked to describe what they like about Camp Fjordmark.

2. If fly-on-the-wall fails to get the material, put the camera away and use an audio-only tape recorder like the ones that radio journalists use. This often produces powerful VO material.

Both of these techniques work well on profiles. Use them on the subject and also with the subject's friends and colleagues whom you'll want to interview to get both information and colour.

> **Best practice:**
> Don't always rely on interviews to get the best sound bites

When Interviews Dominate

Many stories have a "victim;" someone to whom something is happening that may or may not be fair and just. The victim wants something from someone who doesn't want to give it to him. This can be treated as a story with two sides or it can be treated as a *debate* story.

Example: the story is about adopted children of single mothers in Denmark who are not entitled to the standard children's allowance.

Type 1: The Victim's Story

VO: Emma Nielsen is a single mother. She adopted her daughter two years ago from Peru. She feels her daughter is entitled to the children's allowance for single parents because the child is now a Danish citizen. But the authorities don't agree.

Danish Welfare Authority representative: SYNC: *"That's the law. Mothers who adopted did so voluntarily. They're not entitled to this extra support."* (:04)

Emma Nielsen, single mother: SYNC: *"I feel discriminated against. It's not fair. There's no way I can understand this."* (:04)

Emma Nielsen may be justified but all she is doing is complaining. What the story needs is someone who can serve as her advocate and argue her case. The journalist can go to an advocacy agency for adopted children and find a representative. Then the story can be handled as a debate.

Type 2: A Debate Between Equals

VO: Emma Nielsen is a single mother. She adopted her daughter two years ago from Peru. She feels her daughter is entitled to the children's allowance for single parents because the little girl is now a Danish citizen. But the authorities don't agree.

Ping: Danish welfare authority representative: *"That's the law. Single mothers who adopted did so voluntarily. They are not entitled to this extra support."* (:06)

Pong: Adoption advocacy group: *"This law is outdated. More and more children are being adopted and they have economic needs that must be met. A single parent is a single parent regardless of whether it was voluntary or not. Divorces are voluntary, aren't they?"* (:10)

Ping: Danish welfare authority representative: *"Divorce is different from adoption. Children need to be protected after a divorce."* (:06)

Pong: Adoption advocacy group: *" This is a false and arbitrary distinction. A child growing up with a single mother has needs regardless of the circumstances."* (:07)

VO: Emma Nielsen's daughter is too young to realise it but she might become the catalyst for reform.

Pong: Adoption advocacy group: *"The law needs to be reviewed and changed. It's discriminatory to adopted children."* (:05)

Ping: Danish welfare authority representative: *"If people want to change the law, they're welcome to try. This is a democratic country."* (:04)

Journalist in stand-up to camera: *"Children of single parents have special needs and the special allowance is intended to meet these needs. Now there's a coalition of organisations and they're starting to lobby. They want a new law to support adopted children of single parents. The Ministry has agreed to meet with representatives early next week. (Carmen Lopez in Copenhagen).*

Pings and Pongs Must Have the Same Premise

A ping-pong cross cut between two subjects doesn't really work as a debate unless both sides talk about the same issues. The premise of the pong must match the premise of the ping. They must "fit" each other in order to advance the story.

In the first ping, the interview sound bite says: *"That's the law. Mothers who adopted did so voluntarily. They are not entitled to this extra support."*

If the pong had merely said: *"It's discriminatory! And just not fair!"* there would be no debate but a mere exchange of opinions. Consequently, the story would not move forward. Instead, the pong must address the premise of the ping: *"Divorces are also voluntary!"*

Pings and Pongs Should Be of the Same Length

One way to assure balance is to keep the length of the sound bites similar. It doesn't work if the ping is 4 seconds and the pong is 25 seconds

Story Telling Pictures Are Sacrificed

Ping-pong stories use fewer pictures but use the debate to go deeper into the issue. Unless you cover the syncs with pictures, a debate story will probably use fewer pictures than a regular story and can easily evolve into something similar to a radio programme. One way to counter this is by using strong pictures in the context and at the beginning of each premise.

Recording Interviews over the Telephone

Sometimes geographical restrictions require documentation interviews to be recorded over the telephone. These are called "phoners" and they can be effective in spite of their limitations. There are several ways to shoot these. Digital technology is making the possibilities endless. Here are just a few suggestions:

- A medium close-up (MCU) of the telephone with the receiver off the hook. In the upper left hand corner of the screen, show the person's face in a photograph. Identify the speaker with a name and subtitle. Record the interview by placing the microphone near the telephone's speaker.
- Shoot the journalist sitting at a desk talking on the telephone. Frame the shot to allow room for the speaker's photograph. Identify with name and subtitle.
- Use story-telling pictures and freeze frame. Identify the speaker with name and subtitle. The special quality of the audio will tell us it is a "phoner."
- Use graphics that are suitable to the story. Use animation, if possible and appropriate. Identify with name and subtitle.

Never Sacrifice Clean Audio

Recording an interview should take place at a location in which the room tone (or ambient sound) is only 20%. Otherwise, it interferes with the *presence* of the interview. When ambient sound interferes with the VO or the interview, we call it "muddy audio."

Example: the story is about a glass blower and much of his interview is to be used as VO. A big mistake is made when the interview is recorded next to his hot oven. Yes, it is a strong visual but the NATURAL SOUND of blasted heat becomes mixed with his interview, making it almost impossible to understand.

Identify Your Speakers

Check all names for spelling and titles. Each subject should be identified (at least once) by name on the first line and a second line of attribution that shows the person's title or relationship to the story. A formal title tells the viewer if the sync is an expert. If the sync is not an expert but a participant in the story, the second line should tell the viewer the "connection" to the story's angle.

Example: the story is about a political campaign to ratify the European Constitution. Some interviews are experts and others are ordinary voters. If Susan Jones is interviewed as a pro-EU voter, it is not relevant to tell the audience that she is a nurse. The second line, under her name, should read: *Yes on EU Constitution.*

10 The Role of the TV Journalist

Nothing throughout Europe is more controversial in TV journalism than the appropriate role of the journalist. How much, how often should the journalist be seen and heard? Does the presence of the TV reporter enhance the story? Or are they unwanted distractions?

On Camera, in Your Face!

In the USA and the UK, the TV journalist is a magnet for viewers and their extraordinary salaries reflect this. If you are an Anglo-American TV journalist and you're not "good on camera," you're given a behind-the-scenes-job with considerably less pay.

In Denmark, the traditional opinion is that the TV journalist should be invisible, a practice that corresponds to Nordic cultural modesty. Consequently, to be seen in a Danish domestic story was interpreted as unnecessary and therefore, egoistical. This *is* changing, however, slowly but surely. Today we are beginning to see Danish reporters in domestic stories.

Next door in Germany, the appearance of the TV reporter depends on whether the journalist works for a public service station or a commercial one. In the United Kingdom, the TV reporter appears often and usually "tags" the story. Throughout Europe, these on-camera performance practices are culturally determined.[1]

Why Be Seen?

Is there any journalistic reason to be seen on camera? Or is it merely vanity and professional egoism that motivates TV reporters to appear in their stories?

In cultures that value this best practice, the reasons to see the journalist are these:

- It is visual proof that the journalist was there.
- The journalist can give analysis when the story is picture poor.
- The journalist can be a "bridge" between story parts.
- It creates a relationship between the reporter and the viewers who like to see who is talking to them.

Some cultures seem to have a dual policy about on camera and off camera journalists. Norway is one example. In this Nordic culture, some TV journalists are allowed to be on camera and given training to make sure it's successful. Others are heard but never seen.

[1] See Nancy Graham Holm, *Best Practices of Television Journalism in Europe, How Anglo-American on-Camera Styles Violate Cultural Values, Journalism and Mass Communication Educator*, winter, 2006.

Fascination. DOI: 10.1016/B978-0-12-416037-8.00010-9

Nations passionately protect their on-camera and off-camera "best practices," which are obviously derived from deeply rooted cultural values. After that, the rest is rationalisation. When some programme editors want to stop the conversation, all they have to say is: "it's too American!" Of course, this could also mean: "It's too British!" or "It's too Canadian!" or "It's too Australian!" English language cultures share a common practice of showing their TV journalists in action. They do not interpret it as egoistical. They see it as someone doing his job. Part of the job is to be informative. The other part is to lend an element of *fascination* to the story.

TV Journalism Demands Performance Skills

There are a variety of ways in which the journalist appears on camera in a story. Industries who use these techniques believe they enhance fascination by adding energy to the broadcast. To be an on camera TV reporter, however, means accepting the challenge that it requires *performance* skills. Some people are born with natural talent to perform on camera and others need extensive training.

The Alternative Is an Invisible Journalist

Interview subjects never look directly into the lens because *it is implicitly understood that they are speaking to someone.* Who is there? Whom are they talking to? Normally – and this true probably 99.9% of the time – it is the reporter.

This is a conventional practice and it surprises Anglo-American broadcasters why "the other half" is seldom seen in some European TV industries. They know there is a reporter there but they never see who it is.

Consider showing "the other half." Seeing this person confirms that the interview is a conversation and not a monologue. Taking the next step, consider shooting a cutaway on-camera question that can be inserted into the interview during the editing phase. This lends credibility to the report. Here are the five ways the reporter appears in a story:

The "Noddy" Reverse

Traditionally, the reporter's head slightly nods, hence the name "noddy." Today, the preference is a *listening* shot to avoid misinterpretation. This reverse shot is a convenient cutaway to mask jump cuts in an interview. The framing of an interview always leaves space in the frame for the reporter. The cutaway proves that the journalist was really there. (See Chapter 9).

The "Walking and Talking" Setup Shot

This is common practice in Anglo-American broadcast cultures in which the journalist is seen with the subject, waking and talking, sitting and talking or doing something together. It says: *"I was really there."*

The Stand-Up or "Piece to Camera"

This is when the reporter talks directly into the camera lens. It is used either as a bridge between segments of the story or as a conclusion. It gives the reporter the opportunity to give a summary and perspective. Those who use it believe it adds credibility to the story.

The On-Camera Question

The reporter asks a question that is edited into the story. It is controversial among some journalists because with a one-camera shoot, it must be shot after the interview is over, requiring the reporter to ask the question to the camera technician or to a spot on the wall.

Tags

Throughout this book, you have seen parentheses ( ) around the tags at the end of stories, indicating the controversial nature of the practice (cf. pages 52, 54 and 85). Tagging evolved from audience research that said people want to know who's been talking to them. Tagging is not, however, universally desired. Nordic cultures, for example, tend to think it is egoistical. In Denmark TV reporters do tag their stories but only if they are reporting from a foreign country.

When tagging in either a VO or on camera, the reporter says: *"Dominic La Salle, City Hall, Copenhagen."*

This gives two pieces of information: who and where.

Cultures which resist tagging often point out that the viewer already knows who the reporter is because 2 minutes earlier, they read his name on the lower one-third of the screen. To Anglo-Americans, this sounds like an excuse and a rationalisation for not wanting to tag a story. Does the viewer remember the name? Did the viewer even see it during the 4–5 seconds it was visible? What's wrong with telling the viewer again?

Names on the screen are passive identification. Speaking a name is active. Surely, passive identification is inferior to active.

Do I Really Want to Be On Camera?

In nations where modesty is a cultural value, TV journalists who secretly burn to be seen must give themselves permission to learn the required skills. And while they're learning the various performance skills, they must be willing to suffer ridicule from some of their peers in the print and radio media.

There are specialists who train TV journalists and some of them are systematically hired by broadcasting companies to train their reporters. One Canadian trainer asks for total concentration. She calls this skill "the Zen of broadcasting."[2] To be successful, she says, think of RICE.

[2] Halina St. James, *Performing the CBC News.*

- **R**elaxed.
- **I**nterested in what you're saying.
- Connected beyond the camera lens to your viewers.
- Energized because what you give out, you get back.

The essential requirement to being on camera is to believe that you belong there. If you do not believe in yourself, nobody else will.

Getting there, however, is not something you can do by remembering a formula. TV journalists who want to be in cutaways, ask on-cam questions, walk n' talk, do stand-ups and tag their stories, must submit themselves to training and be prepared to practice. By videotaping coaching sessions, one can learn to replace inappropriate habits with dynamic behaviour. Practice in private but practice! There is no substitute for training.

Off Camera: Voice Training Is Recommended

Most stories require a VO. If you want to participate in stories and not be just an arranger behind the scenes, it is wise to get voice training. Using the human voice is not so different from learning to play a musical instrument. Singers know this. They already treat their voices as instruments. High-pitched voices can be offensive. Voices without energy are boring. A "bad voice" can sabotage a good story.

"The Voice of God!"

Within the last few years, an unfortunate cliché has evolved to discredit top down journalists who *report* conventional *information-based* stories. This rather mean spirited concept suggests that it is condescending for a reporter to "talk down" to the audience in a VO. Implicit in this idea of imitating "God's voice" is the belief that *top down* reporting is, by definition, patronising.

This is arrogant nonsense. Such distinctions are foolish and create a false polarity. The relationship between reporting and storytelling is supplementary.

A Misunderstanding About VOs

"We want to produce this without a VO," is what some TV students say. Why? Does it represent some kind of achievement?

This is a misunderstanding. Most TV stories have some kind of VO narration. Some of the best eye-level stories have VOs. Remember the story about assisted suicide in Chapter 7. In Chapter 12 we will hear about a baby whose parents were unable to care for him. Both are eye-level. Both use VOs.

When Is a VO Narration Necessary?

Most TV journalism stories need a VO to guide the viewer, link segments, give the story structure and ultimately to give clarity.

Experience teaches that subjects in videotaped interviews often ramble and get tangential. The same questions that were answered so well over the telephone or in the research interviews lose focus. What was specific now becomes vague. What was charming now becomes banal.

Question: why are journalists necessarily better at narration than their subjects are?

Answer: VO narration is what they've been trained to do. After proper training, TV journalists use their voice to add energy to the VO. In contrast, a subject's *interview used as a VO* can be dull and uninspired. Sometimes it sounds monotonous with little energy.

Finding a Good Talker

Some subjects are very good at telling their own story. Finding a "good talker" is a skill in itself and many TV journalists are good at seeking and finding such people. This is especially true in cultures that encourage extroverted behaviour (American, Italian, Spanish, Irish, Canadian and Australian), but not exclusively. The late Erik Bye of Norway (1926–2004) was a master at finding "good talkers." His roaming reports from around the world ranged from searching America for an old Apache chief to finding an African chieftain from Ghana who answered a message in a bottle.

Is It Ever OK to Editorialize?

Reporting with an opinion is highly controversial and its acceptance will vary from culture to culture. Consider the story about mothers in Scandinavia in Chapter 6. One of the possible angles was *why can't the USA be kinder to mothers?* Just by choosing this angle, a journalist is already expressing an opinion.

But what about the other angle: *the welfare state is good for mothers and children.* Consider the conclusion. Would it be inappropriate for a correspondent reporting to the USA from Denmark to say the following?

T3: A-V tease: *fly-on-the-wall "Bye bye, Niels! Mummy'll see you later!" A mother drops off her child at a Danish kindergarten.* Conclusion VO: There's no doubt that mothers and children have it best under a welfare state. Not only do they get free medical care, they also get economic support to stay home during the first year of the child's life. Their jobs are protected and when they do return to work, their babies get professional childcare in nurseries and kindergartens.

Cut to:

Stand-up (or piece to camera): *"It hasn't always been like this, of course, but in a democracy, people get to have the policies they want. Paid maternity leave and child-care in Scandinavia are the result of political will and a staunch campaign. What about the USA? Why can't America be kinder and more generous to its mothers and children? The question is often asked but there never quite seems to be an answer. In Copenhagen, Denmark... I'm Susannah Graham."*

Reporter-As-Celebrity

One of the negative consequences of commercialising TV news is the inevitable sur-facing of the reporter celebrity. Some reporters project so much in-your-face pres-ence, they inevitably acquire inappropriate influence. America is the best example of this trend but the phenomenon is found in other cultures as well.

In an age of ultra consumerism, there isn't any way to change this except by keep-ing the reporter hidden. The best we can hope for is heightened sensitivity to this media phenomenon. The power to influence comes with responsibility and all we can hope for is that celebrity journalists will take their responsibility to heart.

11 Long Stories

At what point does a story stop being a "short story" and cross the line into the realm of a "long story?" Whatever the answer, it is arbitrary and rather meaningless. The length of a TV journalism story depends on the transmission schedule and the time slot in which it can be broadcast.

What Is a Documentary?

It's hard to define "documentary" because most definitions are restrictive and none fully satisfactory. The word *documentaire* in French, for example, was originally used to describe travel films.

One rather loose definition of *documentary* is "a factual presentation depicting actual events and real people." Some intellectuals and artists would expand the definition to say that a documentary is a documentary *only when it communicates social ideas and values and attempts to bring about change in social and economic conditions.* In other words, a story that attempts to change the status quo. Outstanding examples include: *Hearts and Minds* by Peter Davis (1974); *Harlan County USA* made by Barbara Kopple (1976) *Bowling for Columbine* made by Michael Moore (2002.) and *The High Cost of Low Price* by Robert Greenwald (2005). None is objective. All four have a strong point of view.

Traditional Documentaries Are Subjective

Barbara Kopple's *Harlan County USA* documentary doesn't pretend to objective. Indeed, it gives subjective voice to coalminers on strike against Eastover Mining, owned by Duke Power Company. For four years, Kopple lived periodically among the miners and their families and it is clear that her sympathies lie with the miners and not their bosses. Her camera focuses on the desperate lives of people still living in shacks with no indoor plumbing, working at dangerous jobs with little security and few safety rules. The miners are determined to join the United Mine Workers and the company is determined to break the strike with scabs that are even more desperate than the men with jobs.

Why a News Documentary Is Different

Apparently, documentaries come in all sizes and shapes. It was the application of documentary making to television news journalism, however, that introduced a

Fascination. DOI: 10.1016/B978-0-12-416037-8.00011-0

concept loaded with rules. *Objectivity was assumed. Objectivity was demanded.* This severely separated the traditional point-of-view documentary from the journalistic one.

Perhaps the best definition of a news documentary is a functional one: *the creative and objective treatment of actuality in a story that is longer than a news story.* Whatever definition we use, a documentary is "artistic journalism that may cover a broad range of factual subjects, social, scientific, educational as well as recreational."[1]

Artists or Journalists?

Do we produce for a specialised audience or do we attempt to *communicate* with the masses through target audiences? Is it narrowcasting or broadcasting? Filmmaking is one of the expressive arts and often one encounters documentary makers who have crossed that fine line separating journalists from artists. They have a story they want to tell and they don't really care how many people "like" it. There is a glimmer of divine madness in these artists that makes communication with the masses difficult and unlikely.

Most artists are motivated by a variety of creative impulses running deeper than a desire for the commercial success that comes from a mass audience. Writers write. Musicians compose. Painters paint. Poets write poetry. And some artists use film and videotape to make documentaries about esoteric subjects because it fulfils their artistic personalities. One American filmmaker, Les Blank, has a cult following for making outstanding documentaries about American folk culture. Two of his more famous films are about garlic and women with gaps between their front teeth.[2] Maybe Les Blank is a genius but he is not a journalist. He is an artist.

Journalists, however, do not have the luxury of story telling to a specialised segment of the population because the mission of journalism is to communicate with as many people as possible given the perimeters of the target audience.

Cultural Differences

The documentary is also a victim of cultural differences. In the USA, a serious documentary maker who works outside a television station must raise money for production. When the documentary is finished, relatively few people see it because it is often difficult to get it broadcast on mainstream channels. In a commercial system, numbers count and in the USA the unfortunate attitude prevails that "only intellectuals" want to watch a documentary. Recent developments with cable channels, however, are opening opportunities for American documentary makers and offering the public excellent programming that would never be seen on mainstream television.

---

[1] See Ephraim Katz, *The Film Encyclopedia.* Harper Collins. 1994.
[2] Garlic is as Good as Ten Mothers (1980) and Gap-Tooth Women (1987).

In Europe, the documentary never died. Europeans love documentaries and support them through a wide variety of public funding. Taxpayers fund hundreds a year and public service broadcasting companies air them every night of the week, often in prime time. The audience is Mr. and Mrs. Jones or Hr og Fru Hansen, a mass audience who has stayed loyal while production techniques have evolved and expanded.

The Tool Box

Think of a carpenter's "tool box." Inside are hammers, screwdrivers, drills, saws, different size nails and sandpaper. These are the tools that a carpenter uses to make what he wants. Likewise, in TV documentary making there is a "tool box."

What's the story? Return to our list for short stories. The concepts work just as well for longer stories.

- A problem to be solved
- A challenge to be met
- An obstacle to be overcome
- A threat to be handled
- A decision or choice to be made
- A pressure to be relieved
- A tension to be eased
- A victory to be celebrated
- A kindness to be acknowledged

Treatment?
- Top down Information-based
- Top down feature
- Eye level people story

How many minutes? Chapters?

Voice-over narration? Whose voice?
- The journalist himself/herself
- Another TV professional who is especially good at voicing a track
- A "guest" professional such as movie actor/actress
- Interviews from main subject(s) as VO
- VO read from a prepared script

Photography style?
- *Fly-on-the-wall*
- Constructed
- Re-constructions
- Archive
- Hand-held Tripod Hidden cameras
- *Light* Available? Artificial?
- *Still pictures*? Copies of documents? Headlines in newspapers? Old photographs?

Text boxes?
- Could be used instead of VO.

Interviews?
- Sync sound bites
- Longer syncs through which the main characters tell the story

Role of the journalist?
- Field producer only
- Dominant personality
- Mic-ed off-camera questions
- On camera but not dominating

Graphics?
Music?
Special Effects?
Tempo?
Case Study?

Finding the Case Study

In top down stories, the case study is an *illustration*. In eye level stories, the case study *is* the story. If you need people in either category, the second step in your production plan – after intensive research – is to find them. This is time consuming and requires patience.

Selection is done carefully. The persons involved must be open, intelligent, thoughtful and enthusiastic. If any of these four qualities are absent, your story could easily crash. Ordinary people are not used to a camera crew invading their lives. They can change their minds. They often do and they can change their minds the day before you are scheduled to start shooting the story. Enthusiasm is critically important. If you don't have 110% commitment, stop! Find someone else.

Structure in Information-Based Stories

Structure is a road map. It helps the viewer follow the story and if the story is told with enough fascination, it will be easy to remember. It you muddle it up, putting chapters in the wrong place, the viewer gets confused and has to work harder to follow the story.

Opening

A common structure for an information-based documentary is a blown-up version of the short story:

A-V teaser, angle, context, development and conclusion.

Such stories also follow the TTT model. A common "teaser" is a summary of what is to come, using brief sound bites from interviews to introduce the story's principal themes. It is perfectly acceptable to use the same sound bites later in the body of the story, often in an expanded version.

Body

Careful consideration must be given to the order of chapters. Attention to dramatic unfolding is critical. It can follow an uphill development towards a dramatic climax or it can use a "wave model" that has sub-units of self-contained dramatic developments. In the wave model, each chapter would end with a mini-climax.

Issues are often best treated by themes, building the story from the least impressive to the most. Consider chronology; sometimes it is effective such as a fly-on-the-wall reportage of a particular process, e.g., building a dam; developing a new kindergarten; following a political campaign. Daily time, however, is arbitrary and not inherently dramatic. A common error for beginners is to think that "a-day-in-the-life-of" is inherently interesting. It is not.

Transitions Between Chapters

These are the road signs on the highway. They tell you where the next stop is. There are several ways to communicate that you are leaving one chapter and going to another.

- A-V transitions
- Dip to black and up again with audio L cut
- Picture with graphics
- Thematic breakers (bumpers)
- Black screen with text

The most aesthetic introduction to the next chapter is the first option, an A-V transition. This uses the medium to its best potential.

Thematic breakers should never be absolutely identical. Repetition can become an irritation instead of an enhancement. When possible, change the base picture. Be careful with music. Hearing the same rift over and over again might be irritating. A compelling rift that "buttons" however, can enhance fascination.

Using text on a black screen is old fashioned and not recommended. Dipping to black and then introducing audio on an L cut is better.

Ending

There are exceptions, but usually there is some type of summary, bringing the audience full circle so that the relevance of the story is completely understood. Like the introduction, it is a small percentage of the story. Without this summary it is sometimes hard to remember the principal premise of the story. Unlike the short news story, however, here the piece can end on a juicy sound bite from one of the interviews.

Structure in Identification Stories

Top down features and eye level people stories do not have to follow the strict TTT model because they are not driven by information but identification. These stories need chapters, however and a dramatic unfolding. Thematic chapters work well for both types. Simple chronology is not advised. Identification stories rely heavily on the case studies and if possible, it is wise to have more than one. Chapters can then be divided thematically between the different people. For obvious reasons, experts are seldom seen in identification stories.

Examples of Categories and Styles

Documentary makers pick and choose techniques from their "tool box" to fit the subject. In broad terms, a documentary can be educational, traditional or news-style.

The Private Life of Plants, (BBC, 1995). This is a top down educational documentary, featuring David Attenborough as the authoritative story teller and it is his personality that drives the story. Time-lapse photography shows us how plants grow, flower and struggle to survive. The budget was big. The tempo is slow. The photography is breathtakingly beautiful.

Grownup Kids, (Danmarks Radio, 1996*)*. This is an eye level documentary by Danish journalist, Ulrik Holmstrup. It is a portrait of children who must grow up fast in order to take over the management of their families when one or both parents are dysfunctional. Two case studies tell the story. The journalist is invisible yet interactive and subjective by asking mic-ed off camera questions to the children. The voice-over, however, is objective from another person. The story is told through a blend of fly-on-the-wall and constructed segments with VO from the children. There is only one expert. The photography is pretty with symbolic pictures of innocence and light, using country landscapes and a sunny blue sky. The opening and closing segments are constructed to give us a visual metaphor: a little girl is riding a bicycle that is too big for her. At the end, she finally falls off, leaving the bicycle on the ground, its wheels spinning.

Return to Freetown, *(CNN, 2002)*. This is a top down news documentary by African journalist, Sorious Samura. He returns to Sierra Leone and is both an observer and interactive. This time his goal is to locate the families of three child soldiers and bring them home. Fly-on-the-wall reportage is blended with many stand-ups from Samura. The voice-over content is subjective because he is part of the story. No experts. The photography is not spectacular but the story, told chronologically, is immensely engaging.

Untitled, *(France, 1994)*. This is a portrait and an eye level documentary. It is the story of two French transvestite prostitutes that is told not through pictures but through interviews. Over 70% of the story is on-camera conversations with an invisible inter-active journalist who follows the two prostitutes in Paris, asking off camera, mic-ed questions. There is some fly-on-the-wall reportage and few constructed scenes. The transitions are conventional and the general production is conservative. Some critics might call this programme a "radio" show but the faces and body language of the case studies hold a lot of information.

Heart of the Angel (Australia, 2001). Molly Dineen, producer and director, made this eye level documentary before the renovation of the 100-year-old Angel tube station on the London metro. The film charts 48 hours in a life of the people who work there. Ray Stocker is a man who hates change and remembers fondly the days when chandeliers hung on the platform of the Angel. Ticket-seller Derek Perkins is both a wit and philosopher to the bemused passengers who file past his window. At midnight, gangs of women called 'fluffers' get down on their hands and knees to clean human hair of the tracks. The invisible journalist is reflective and also inter-active with off cam mic-ed questions.

Everest, (Mac Gillivray Freeman Film, 1998). This is a classical lyrical documentary that mixes eye level with top down reporting. It tells the story about a team of climbers who believe that dreams can be attained through incredible effort and risk. The voice-over narrative is objective from movie star Liam Neeson, who is restricted to observation since he did not climb Mt. Everest and was not a part of the expedition. Other VOs come from the interviews and also from scripted text that is read by the participants from a studio. Some segments are breathtaking and fly-on-the-wall at its best.

The Road to Oklahoma (CNN, 1995). This is a USA top down multi-part news documentary about the 1995 terrorist attack on the US Federal Building in Oklahoma City. Each mini-doc is about 9:00-12:00, using both constructed pictures and fly-on-the-wall. NATURAL SOUND tells almost 30% of the story. Typical of an American news-style documentary, the tempo is fast paced with an editing ratio of 2-3 sec./edit. The journalist observes and is present on camera in a stand-up.

Elizabeth R (BBC, 1992). This is produced as a traditional top down documentary with a high percentage of fly-on-the-wall reportage. It is a portrait of England's Queen Elizabeth II to show her life over the course of a year. There is both an objective narrator and a subjective VO from Queen Elizabeth herself that were taken from interviews. Her Royal Majesty is never seen in SYNCS since all segments from interviews are used VO. It is pure observation. Some critics wonder if it is journalism or public relations.

The Essential Denmark (BBC, 1993.) This is a traditional top down documentary and a portrait of Denmark, produced by the British to introduce Denmark to the other members of the European Union. It has several distinct chapters, each with a specific theme made by a different journalist. In one chapter, it uses dramatic reconstruction to show how Danish Jews were smuggled to Sweden during WW II. All the chapters use constructed pictures with minimal fly-on-the-wall reportage. In addition, the programme uses chromakey photography to frame the interviews, extensive use of music and electronic techniques to enhance the drama of history. It is essentially observational with an objective voice from an invisible narrator.

Fleeing to Europe (Danmarks Radio, 1991). This is a traditional top down documentary using outstanding fly-on-the-wall reportage and interviews. There are virtually no constructed pictures. It is pure observation with an invisible journalist who links the segments in VO. The transitions from one theme to the other use chapter headings in text graphics over black, a technique borrowed from print journalism that is by definition picture poor and old fashioned. The power in this conservatively produced documentary is in the information: *there is human time bomb waiting to explode! Immigration from the have-not nations will be the most important issue in the 21st century.*

12 Ethical Considerations for Eye Level Documentaries

Eye level features are high in identification and indeed, essentially fascinating. *Storytelling* as a genre is fundamentally more engaging than *reporting* because it is far more emotional than it is intellectual.

As humans, we enjoy our emotions because they make us feel human but perhaps, this is exactly why some traditional journalists remain suspicious of eye level journalism. Where are the boundaries? Where is the discipline? What are the rules? Eye level storytelling on television is not without ethical considerations.

The first thing you might hear about eye level storytelling is that a suspension of critical judgment is dangerous. When stories are so fascinating that viewers lose themselves in the story, they also lose their ability to think critically. There is a thin line between persuasion and propaganda.

Secondly, without a strong *case study*, the story cannot work. "Casting the character" is what narrative print journalists call it, and it requires time and luck. Ernest-Karl Aschmoneit, the engineer who chose assisted suicide (Chapter 7) was perfect for an eye level story. One can well imagine the journalists' excitement when they heard about him. One *New York Times* Pulitzer prize-winning journalist took several months to find the "right family" to tell her story about crack cocaine addiction in a Chicago tenement neighbourhood.[1] Such a lengthy search is a luxury.

Best practice:
Be realistic!
Do you have time to find a suitable case study?

One experience in 2003 with a television graduation project at DSMJ illustrates how a deadline interferes with the success of an assignment. The story was about a hospice and what it is like to die in a supportive environment instead of the sterile atmosphere of a hospital.

The student journalists found two case studies and got their permission to follow them to their death. They spent many days at the hospice but neither of the case studies "cooperated." One person's health improved and he was sent home. The second person lingered at the edge of death and grew increasingly irritated about the presence of the camera. She stopped cooperating and sent them away. She died but long after deadline.

---

[1] From a presentation by Isabel Wilkerson, October 10, 2003 at a conference on narrative journalism, sponsored by *Center for Journalistik og Efteruddannelse*, Århus.

Fascination. DOI: 10.1016/B978-0-12-416037-8.00012-2

The story "failed" and the students didn't get the grade they had hoped for. A fair amount of their examination was spent talking about the risks implicit in the choice of their story.

Examples of stories whose case studies may be difficult to find:

- Ecstasy, the popular recreational drug
- Binge drinking
- Sexual behaviour of the handicapped
- Prison-based homosexuality
- Dying: from cancer or another disease
- Domestic violence
- Child pornography
- Human trafficking for prostitution

Thirdly, getting people's cooperation doesn't always come without extreme effort. Getting the enthusiastic cooperation of the case study requires skill and patience. In the absence of enthusiasm and full-fledged support, the situation can become exploitative.

At a narrative journalism conference in Denmark, one Pulitzer Prize journalist gave a lengthy and detailed description of how she persuaded her chosen family to cooperate, a process that resulted in three pages of note taking.

She encouraged narrative journalists to find someone in crisis but to wait until just the right moment to ask for their participation. She drew a diagram to show when the person would be most receptive. Persuasion? Or manipulation? In the final analysis, if the story can shed light in a dark corner of society that results in the improvement of lives, some degree of manipulation might be forgiven.

Fourthly, do case studies always know what they're doing when they agree to cooperate? Surely persuasive journalists can get what they want, but what if the very best case study is someone with low intelligence? Is their permission and willingness to cooperate ethically valid? This consideration is particularly true of television.

In 1998, a documentary was produced in Denmark to examine parental rights vs. the rights of a newborn child. *Born to Lose* by Lars Høj became a showcase example of a people story.

Anni gives birth to Jørn. The baby's father, Bjarne, is present and in the first three minutes of the documentary, they look just like any new family. Soon it is painfully obvious, however, that Anni and Bjarne are mentally sub-normal. The documentary follows the baby's first four months and we watch Anni and Bjarne angrily interact with patient, long-suffering Danish health workers who try to teach them now to nurture their little son. They cannot take proper care of their baby, however, and for the better part of an hour, the viewer watches and cringes as baby Jørn's development steadily deteriorates.

Screening this documentary gets mixed reactions. Some viewers like it very much. Others say they feel like *voyeurs,* watching immature, unpleasant people without dignity or awareness stumble through life while threatening the wellbeing of an infant.

Watching the documentary is not easy viewing. It is, however, far more effective in getting its message across than a traditional top-down documentary with a string of experts discussing incompetent parenting. The ethical question, however, haunts the consciences of some professional journalists. Does it matter that the inhumane and emotionally stunted behaviour of Anni and Bjarne is put on show? Did they know what they were saying yes to when they agreed to cooperate? Does it matter?

Fifthly, narrative journalism in print is not necessarily invasive. The information might be in the details but the details are described in words. A TV camera and a microphone, however, are unavoidably invasive. If the information is in the details, it means that the details of someone's life must be photographed and recorded. Does the case study candidate really understand what it means to allow a TV camera crew into one's life? Even if the photography is fly-on-the-wall, the camera is there. Every single day. It cannot be escaped.

Some case study candidates will say yes to this invasion because they love the attention. Others will destroy the project by "walking," often at the last minute. Indeed, many *people story* documentaries have been hijacked by case studies that change their minds about participating. Can we blame them? Think about the dying woman in the hospice story. It could not have been very pleasant to have two strangers hanging around.

People Stories Need a Lot of Footage

Lastly, a final consideration that is merely technical and not ethical. Eye level stories shoot a lot of tape. While shooting ratios on a basic information-based story can be rather low, maybe even 3:1 if well organised, people stories use fly-on-the-wall reportage, requiring enormous amounts of tape; a 100:1 ratio or even higher is not unusual. The consequences of this are obvious.

Glossary

angle: the focus of the story; what it is that you want to tell the viewer. Topics are not angles. Topics can have many different angles. (Chapters 4, 6)

archive: pictures and sound that were previously used but are relevant to your current story as file footage. (Chapter 4)

aspect ratio: 3:4 is normal TV. NDTV is 3:5.3

A-V script: the conventional design for a script with audio on the right side and video on the left. (Chapter 6)

A-V sound bite: natural sound with pictures (Chapters 1–3, 5–9)

A-V tag: using natural sound and pictures to end a story after the journalist has signed off. (Chapter 6)

A-V teases or transitions: audio-video; pictures and natural sound. They introduce a story, serve as transitions between points or chapters and generally add fascination. (Chapters 2, 3, 5–7)

axis line: an imaginary straight line projected from the tip of the camera lens through the centre of the subject and beyond. Crossing the line results in false reverses in the action. (See Z axis) (Chapter 9)

BBI: "boring but important" means the story is picture poor and not obviously suitable for television. The opposite of "sexy story." (Chapters 4, 6)

bites: short segments of interviews. (See A-V sound bite) (Chapters 1–3, 8, 9)

boom mic: microphone held on a long telescopic boom moved skilfully by a sound technician. (Chapter 10)

buttons: when music comes to melodic resolution, such as the end of a phrase. (Chapter 11)

catch light: reflected light in eyes that enhances engagement. (Chapter 9)

chocolate rule: a short-hand description of over-used intensity. (Chapter 9)

chromakey: CSO: colour separation overlay. A technical method of electronically replacing a single colour (usually blue) with a second picture or image.

close-up: CU: a shot that fills the screen. (Chapter 3)

colour: a type of sound bite from an interview that gives opinion, not facts. (See support) (Chapter 6)

conclusion: the third and last part of an information-based story (T3) in which a summary is made of the story's angle. (Chapter 6)

context: the background of a story that makes the rest of it make sense. (Chapter 6)

continuity: the assembly of shots that clarify an event. (Chapter 3)

current affairs: journalism stories that go beyond the basic questions of who, what, when and where found in news bulletins but also ask *why*. The lengths vary from 2:30 to 4:00–8:00 and include news documentaries. (Chapter 6)

cutaway: a shot in a picture sequence that is used to mask an edit. (Chapters 3, 6, 10)

development: the middle part (T2) of an information-based story in which information is given systematically in points. (Chapter 6)

dissolve: where one picture is faded out and another faded in simultaneously. (Chapters 3, 6)

editing: tertiary motion; the assembly of pictures and sound. Editors strive both to create illusion and to reconstruct reality, as well as to guide viewers' emotional responses. (Chapters 2, 3, 5–7, 9, 11)

establishing shot: ES. A picture used to introduce the viewer to the story's locale or to the story itself. Usually a wide shot but not necessarily the very first shot in the sequence. (Chapter 4)

eye level: refers to stories that are told through people and not a reporter. (See people stories) (Chapters 4, 7)

fascination: one of the three elements of current affairs journalism, required for emotional engagement. (Chapters 1–12)

fly-on-the-wall: a type of reportage in which the camera watches the action unnoticed. (Chapters 3–5, 7)

focus: the premise of the story; the angle. (Chapters 4–7)

fx: abbreviation for "sound effects." (Chapter 2)

general specific general: corresponds to TTT in information-based stories. (Chapter 6)

good talker: a subject who is a good storyteller. (Chapter 10)

hard news: important information. (Chapter 4)

Harry Potter edit: an edit in which the subject crosses time and space at the speed of light. Any movement that could never happen in real life. (Chapters 3, 6, 10)

headroom: framing a person's face in a MCU or CU that allows for frame space at the top of the head. (Chapters 3 and 9)

human interest: a soft news item that is interesting to the viewer but of no great significance or importance. (Chapter 4)

illustrative video: separate shots of video linked to each sentence or paragraph of a script with little regard for continuity in subject matter or consecutiveness from one shot to the next. (Chapter 3)

identification: one of the elements of current affairs journalism, required to emotionally engage the viewer. (See fascination) (Chapters 1, 7, 8, 12)

information: one of three elements of current affairs journalism, conventionally considered dominant over the other two. (See identification and fascination) (Chapters 1, 4–7)

jump cut: an action that is perceived to jump unnaturally into a new position on the screen. In interviews, the spastic movement of subjects. (See Harry Potter edit) (Chapters 3, 5–7, 10)

L cut: in digital editing when we hear something before we see it. (Chapters 2–4, 6, 7)

long shot: LS: a full view of a subject. (Chapter 3)

medium shot: MS: any shot that begins to isolate it from the overall environment. They can be composed in several different sizes. (Chapter 3)

motivated: any secondary shot (pan, tilt, zoom, truck) that contributes to the understanding of the story. (Chapter 3)

muddy audio: when ambient sound interferes with the interview or VO. (Chapter 9)

natural sound: sounds from the environment that serve to heighten the viewer's sense of realism. The British call it *actuality*. (Chapters 1–12)

noddy: a cutaway to mask an edit in an interview. This is a British term for a reverse shot of the journalist listening. (Chapters 3, 10)

package: an edited, self-contained videotape report of a news event or feature, not requiring the studio presenter to tell 15% of the story. (Chapters 1, 4, 6)

pan: a type of secondary motion in which the lens moves horizontally. (Chapter 3)

people stories: an alternative to conventional reporting (top down) in which stories are told through people's own experience (eye level). (Chapters 4, 7–9)

phoner: a recorded telephone interview. (Chapter 9)

Piaf: to edit music with lyrics over the top of VO or snatches of interview. (Chapter 2)

piece-to-camera: information given by a reporter on location directly into the camera. This is a British term for what Americans call a stand-up. (Chapter 10)

points: the focus of each chapter in the development segment (T2) of information-based stories. (Chapters 1, 6)

pulse points: words that are read with extra energy in a VO that give rhythm to the narration. (Chapter 3)

primary motion: event motion in front of the camera. (Chapter 3)

reportage: what the TV photographer shot at a specific event where the action cannot be controlled. (Chapter 3)

room tone: the ambient sound peculiar to each separate environment that is inserted into editing to prevent sound dropouts. (Chapter 2)

secondary motion: camera motion including pan, tilt, truck and zoom. (Chapter 3)

sequence: a series of shots that produce a continuous, uninterrupted flow of action that communicates a sense of experience. (Chapter 3)

sequential photography: a family of pictures with the father as LS and Es, the mother as a variety of medium shots and the children as a variety of close-ups. (Chapter 3)

sexy story: a story with instant audience appeal. (Chapter 4)

sharply angled: the middle part of an information-based story in which all points are subordinate to the angle and take the story deeper not wider. (Chapter 6)

shopping list: all the illustrative pictures that are needed to go with segments of VO. (Chapter 3)

shooting ratio: the ratio of footage recorded in the field to that which is used in the finished story. (Chapters 3, 11, 12)

signposting: a model for structure that highlights the angle at the top of the story, develops the angle in the middle of the story and finally repeats the premise at the end. (See TTT) (Chapter 6)

sound bite: a brief portion of an interview. May also refer to a snatch of natural sound from a location. (Chapters 2, 5, 6, 8, 9)

stand-up: information given by a reporter on location facing the camera. The British call this *piece to camera*. (Chapter 10)

storytelling: an alternative to reporting, stories are told not through a reporter but through people. (See people stories) (Chapters 4, 7, 12)

support: a type of sound bite from an interview that gives facts. (See colour) (Chapters 6, 9)

sync: a segment from an interview of any length. The term comes from the synchronized movements of the subject's lips with the sound. (See sound bite) (Chapters 2, 3, 9)

30–70 principle: in information-based stories, the proportion of interview bites to VO narration from the reporter. (Chapters 4, 6)

TTT: signposting: tell me what you want to tell me; tell me; tell me what you told me. (See general-specific-general) (Chapter 6)

tag: to end a story by identifying oneself and the location. (Chapter 10)

tertiary motion: editing rhythm. (Chapters 3, 6)

top down: refers to stories that are reported from field journalists. (See eye level) (Chapters 4–6)

treatment: a plan for how a story is to be told. (Chapter 4)

voice of God: a negative and disparaging reference to top down reporting, implying that it is condescending. (Chapter 10)

voice over: information spoken by the reporter over the top of pictures. (Chapter 2)

wallpaper: pictures with little meaning. (Chapter 3)

Z **axis:** an index and motion vector that points or moves toward or away from the camera. (Chapter 3)

zig-zag: in top down features, the story line might move in a forward-backward-forward motion, weaving elements into a whole. This is not allowed in information-based stories. (Chapters 4–6)

About the Author

Nancy Graham Holm was Department Head at The Danish School of Media and Journalism from 1991 to 2007 after coming to Denmark with 20 years of experience in broadcast journalism in the San Francisco Bay Area. Her last position was Editorial Director at KPIX (CBS affiliate) where she was the recipient of four regional Emmys for current affairs programming. She holds an M.A. in history from the University of California, Berkeley and resides in Aarhus, Denmark where she continues to work independently in both video and print.

Bibliography

This book is a thin slice of the TV journalism pie. Students and instructors who wish to go both deeper and wider into the vast universe of TV broadcasting have an extensive library from which to draw. Here are just a few sources to supplement this book and hopefully to validate it.

Boyd, Andrew. *Broadcast Journalism*, 5th edition London: Focal Press, 2001.

Everton, Neil. *Making Television News*. England: Reuters Foundation, 1999.

Everton, Neil. *The VJ Handbook*. Canada: CBC; 1999.

Holm, Nancy Graham. Amerikansk indflydelse på dansk tv-journalistik, *Nye nyheder*. CFJE, 1999.

Holm, Nancy Graham. Comparing American and European Television: Radio with Pictures. *P.O.V. A Danish Journal of Film Studies*. December 2000;12.

Holm, Nancy Graham. Best Practices of Television Journalism in Europe: How Anglo-American On-Camera Styles Violate Cultural Values; Denmark as a Case Study, *Journalism and Mass Communication Educator*. Winter, 2006.

Holm, Nancy Graham. Narrative Journalism: Subjectivity, No Longer a Dirty Word. *P.O.V. A Danish Film Journal of Film Studies*, December 2006.

Mills, Jenni. *The Broadcast Voice*. England: Focal Press; 2004.

Ray, Vin. *The Television News Handbook*. London: Macmillan; 2003.

St. James, Halina. The CBC News. CBC Learning and Development, Toronto, ON: 2002.

Shook, Frederick. *Television News Writing*. New York: Longman; 1994.

Shook, Frederick, John Larson and John DeTarsio. *Television Field Production and Reporting*, (Boston, Allyn and Bacon, 2012).

Thompson, Rick. *Writing for Broadcast Journalists*. England: Routledge: 2005.

Townley, James. *The Best Editing Goes Unnoticed*. NPPA Workshop; OK: 1995.

Whittaker, Ron. Video Field Production, 2nd edition. America: Mayfield Publishing Company, 1996.

Winston, Brian. *Lies, Damn Lies and Documentaries*. London: BFI, 2000.

Zettl, Herbert. *Sight, Sound and Motion*, 6th edition. Wadswort, Belmont, California, 2012.

Zettl, Herbert. *Television Production Handbook*, 11th edition. Wadsworth, Belmont, California, 2012.

Lightning Source UK Ltd.
Milton Keynes UK
UKOW020857210112

185789UK00001B/13/P